THE
SOCIAL SECURITY
Answer Book

Practical Answers to Over 200 Questions on Social Security

STANLEY A. TOMKIEL III

SPHINX® PUBLISHING
AN IMPRINT OF SOURCEBOOKS, INC.®
NAPERVILLE, ILLINOIS
www.SphinxLegal.com

Second Edition, 2008

Published by: **Sphinx® Publishing, An Imprint of Sourcebooks, Inc.®**

Naperville Office
P.O. Box 4410
Naperville, Illinois 60567-4410
630-961-3900
Fax: 630-961-2168
www.sourcebooks.com
www.SphinxLegal.com

This publication is designed to provide accurate and authoritative information in regard to the subject matter covered. It is sold with the understanding that the publisher is not engaged in rendering legal, accounting, or other professional service. If legal advice or other expert assistance is required, the services of a competent professional person should be sought.

From a Declaration of Principles Jointly Adopted by a Committee of the American Bar Association and a Committee of Publishers and Associations

This product is not a substitute for legal advice.

Disclaimer required by Texas statutes

Library of Congress Cataloging-in-Publication Data
Tomkiel, Stanley A.
  The social security answer book / by Stanley A. Tomkiel, III. -- 1st ed.
      p. cm.
  Includes index.
  ISBN-13: 978-1-57248-587-7 (pbk. : alk. paper)
  ISBN-10: 1-57248-587-6 (pbk. : alk. paper)
   1. Social security--Law and legislation--United States--Popular works. I. Title.
  KF3650.T66 2007
  344.7302'3--dc22
                                                      2007004307

Printed and bound in the United States of America.

VP — 10 9 8 7 6 5 4 3 2 1

Contents

Introduction

As a former Social Security claims representative and as an attorney, I have been handling Social Security questions for more than twenty-five years. In that time I have had thousands and thousands of questions posed to me from members of the public, clients, attorneys, accountants and professionals of various kinds. Many people, including professionals, have difficulty even forming a question because they lack basic insight into the Social Security system – what it is intended to cover, and not to cover. There are so many various social programs that it is easy to get confused.

To provide a meaningful response to a question, it is important to understand the thought process of the questioner. For this reason, I have included in this book the *actual* questions of real people. I have constructed my answers in a way that explains not only the correct information, but also the possible misconception, if there is one. I have tried to provide a complete answer; even if that has required a lengthy response.

All too often the official pamphlets and question-and-answer formats, commonly encountered, have canned questions that are designed to provide a vehicle for giving a certain tidbit of information. This makes for very boring reading. In this book I have used real questions from real people about various areas of Social Security. Some of the questions may appear peculiar. Some of the questions may appear as if they came from a soap opera. I assure you that all the questions are real and from real people. The only editing done was for grammatical reasons.

To make the best use of this book you should first think about what type of a question it is that you have. If it deals with the process of getting the benefits or how much money you get, then you should go to Chapter 7 for Applying for Benefits and Chapter 8 for Benefit Payments. If your question relates to benefits for the covered worker, you should look at Chapter 2 for Disability or Chapter 1 for Retirement. If you are looking for information for benefits for dependents or survivors, then you would go to Chapters 3, 5, and 6. Chapter 4 deals with Medicare, while Chapters 9 and 10 deal with more general things like the Social Security tax, number, card, and identity theft.

These questions have been gathered from inquiries sent to me by e-mail from around the country. I can answer for free only a fraction of the questions I receive, however, I post the answers on my website. I choose questions that have a wide application so that many readers can benefit. If you would like to submit a question or read questions from others with my answers, or for the latest Social Security information, visit my website at:

www.socialsecuritybenefitshandbook.com

Chapter 1 — RETIREMENT

The core of the Social Security system is the retirement program. This was the original intent of Social Security and encompasses today the greatest number of beneficiaries. It is the largest of the three programs of retirement, survivors, and disability. The general intent for retirement benefits was originally to provide a replacement for income lost due to age and its attendant restrictions on earning capacity. In recent years, this has been modified to become an age entitlement program, by eliminating any earnings restrictions for those of Full Retirement Age, which is being gradually increased for those born after 1937.

The increase is going in increments of two months according to a schedule by year of birth. For those born in 1938, Full Retirement Age is 65 and two months, for those born in 1939, it is age 65 and four months, and it continues to increase for those born in later years. The retirement age levels off at age 66 for those born from 1943 through 1954.

It continues to rise again at the same two-month-per-year rate for those born in 1955 and later until the Full Retirement Age ultimately becomes age 67 for those born in 1960 and later. A beneficiary may still collect a retirement benefit beginning as early as age 62, but the rate of reduction will be greater, due to the later Full Retirement Age. Previously, the full age reduction was 20% at age 62 and under the revised law, it will be 30% at age 62 for those born in 1960 and later.

The following questions and answers address concerns about:
- *how and when to apply for the retirement benefits;*
- *how to maximize payable benefits;*
- *effect of earnings on those benefits; and,*
- *the effect of other types of income.*

Q My husband will be officially retired April 1st of this year and is leaving under early retirement. He would like to work again to subsidize his income, but does not want to lower his future Social Security benefits. Another person told us that his Social Security benefit will be based on his last five years of work history. Since he is five years away from drawing his Social Security, just exactly what can he do to subsidize his income and not hurt his future benefit?

He made over $16 an hour from his employer where he worked for thirty-six years. Naturally, if you begin another job (since jobs are so few and far between), the pay would be on the order of $7 to $9 an hour.

What is he allowed to do in order not to hurt the future benefit he will receive based on his thirty-six years of employment with the company? He sure doesn't want to begin another job at a much lower pay scale and have his Social Security benefit reduced due to working for a lot less pay in the next five years.

A It is a *common misconception* that Social Security benefits are based on the last five years of earnings. Actually, Social Security benefits are based on earnings over a forty-year period. The lowest five years are dropped and the average earnings are taken over the remaining thirty-five years. The thirty-five years do not have to be consecutive and a later year can be substituted for an earlier year if there are earnings after retirement. In your husband's case, if he stops working now, his benefits will not be lowered if he works even part time between now and the time he becomes 62.

In fact, if his earnings in a post-retirement year are higher than one of his earlier years of earnings, then his part-time work may actually *increase* his Social Security benefit. So you can tell him to go ahead and work and it will not lower his Social Security benefits at all. If anything, it *may* increase them.

Q **If you are drawing out of your IRA, is this counted with the wages you may be earning if you continue to work a few hours when you start drawing your Social Security?**

A No. Payments received from your retirement plans, whether IRAs, Keogh's or other company pension plans, will have no effect on your Social Security retirement benefits.

Q **My husband will reach full retirement age in October. He is now collecting a retirement from the U.S. Air Force reserves. He works at the post office, but would like to work and collect his Social Security at the same time. How will the air force retirement affect the amount that he receives from Social Security? Also, our children are 13 and 16—will they be able to collect?**

A Your husband will be eligible for his Social Security regardless of other pensions he may receive. He can work, but if his earnings exceed the *annual exempt amount* for the year, then he will lose $1 in Social Security benefits for every $3 over the annual exempt amount. This exempt amount varies depending on your age. For those who attain full retirement age in 2007, the annual exempt amount is $34,440. Furthermore, the only earnings that count are months before he attains full retirement age.

For Example:
If his annual earnings for January through September are less than $34,440, he will be able to receive his full Social Security benefits.

The children will also be entitled to receive benefits until they turn 18. Furthermore, as the mother of a child under 16, you will also be able to collect as a young wife. Your entitlement to young wife's benefits will end when your youngest child turns 16.

Q **How much money can you earn while drawing Social Security after full retirement age?**

A You can earn as much as you care to *after* reaching full retirement age. *Full Retirement Age* earnings will not affect benefit payments. For the year you attain *Full Retirement Age*, you lose $1 in benefits for every $3 over the exempt amount of wages earned before attaining *Full Retirement Age*. For the year 2007, the annual exempt amount is $34,440. If you earn $34,440 or less in the year you reach full retirement age, your benefits for the entire year will be unaffected. For years after the year you have reached full retirement age, there is no limit whatsoever.

Q **In February, I applied for retirement benefits because I wanted to retire from my present job on May 1st. I will be 64 in June. I was told that I had to apply at least three months in advance to start receiving benefits in May. Much to my surprise, I started receiving my check in February and now one in March. Will I be penalized for these benefits even though I specifically stated that I was not retiring until May 1st and am still working? I am very puzzled by these checks.**

A You are receiving your benefits even before you retire because your annual earnings for the four months you are working in 2007 must be less than the annual exempt amount. $12,960 is the annual exempt amount because you are under *Full Retirement Age*. For the year 2007, as long as your annual earnings for the year are less than this amount, you can receive benefits for all months in the year during which you are over 62.

Q I received a Social Security statement, which gave me a benefit I would receive if I was to retire at age 62. I would like to know how much of a benefit I could receive at age 55. Thank you.

A There is no retirement benefit payable until you are at least 62 years old throughout the month. You may be eligible for a disability benefit if you are totally disabled and your survivors may be entitled to benefits in the event of your death. But there is no retirement benefit payable to you at 55.

Q Does gender make any difference in the amount of Social Security benefits paid or is it entirely based on earnings?
Is there a penalty if both husband and wife are drawing Social Security because they are married or do single persons get a better benefit?

A There are no longer any sex distinctions in Social Security law, although at one time there were. The amount of retirement benefits is based exclusively on the amount of earnings and the age of the worker.

There is no penalty for a husband and wife who are both drawing Social Security because they are married. In fact, a wife (or a husband) may collect a benefit on the spouse's account if her (or his) benefit on her or his work record is lower. If both spouses have earnings on their own accounts, both will receive benefits based on their own earnings. But if one spouse's benefit is less than half of the other's, additional spouse's benefits are payable to bring the spouse up to one half of the higher spouse's benefit amount.

Q How much money can you earn in one year working part time and receive Social Security at age 62?

A It does not matter whether you work part time or full time. If you are under *Full Retirement Age*, then for the year 2007 you can earn up to $12,960 without any effect on your Social Security benefits. If you earn over this amount, you will lose $1 of Social Security benefits for every $2 over this annual limit. Beginning with the year you reach full retirement age you will be able to earn much more (for the year 2007 the limit is $34,440 per year) and if your earnings exceed that amount, you will lose $1 for every $3 over that limit.

Q At what age can you begin receiving Social Security? Is it still at age 62? I realize the amount won't be as much as it would be if you waited till you were 65 or 66 to start receiving benefits, but I need to know if I can still get it at age 62. Thank you.

A You can still get it beginning with the first month in which you are age 62 throughout the month. For most people this means the first month of entitlement will be the month after their 62nd birthday. However, if you were born on the first or second day of the month, you will be considered age 62 throughout that month.

Since 2000, the *Full Retirement Age* has been increased. For those born in 1937 or earlier, 65 is the *Full Retirement Age*. If you begin your benefits at age 62, they will be reduced by 20%. Beginning with those born in 1938, the *Full Retirement Age* is increasing in two-month increments for each year up. So, for a person born in 1938, the *Full Retirement Age* is 65 and two months. For someone born in 1940, it is age 65 and six months. You can still receive the benefit at age 62, but the reduction will be greater because you are that many more months below *Full Retirement Age*.

For persons born from 1943 to 1954, *Full Retirement Age* is age 66, and the full reduction at age 62 will be 25%. For people born in 1955 and later, the *Full Retirement Age* will continue to increase in two-month increments each year until it reaches age 67 for those born in 1960 and later. The full age reduction at 62 for those persons will be 30% off the full retirement benefit.

Q When I turn 65, can I apply for and receive my Social Security benefits and continue to work full time?

A Your earnings in the year you reach *Full Retirement Age* will affect your Social Security benefits, but only if those earnings for the months before you reach *Full Retirement Age* exceed the annual exempt amount. That figure for 2007 is $34,440. If earnings for those months exceed that sum, then you will lose $1 in benefits for every $3 over that limit. After the year you reach *Full Retirement Age*, your earnings will have no effect on your Social Security benefits. You may continue to work and earn as much as you like and still collect your full benefits without penalty.

Q I am a 53-year-old resident of the state of Minnesota. What is the earliest possible date I can start collecting Social Security, even with the penalty?

A You can collect Social Security retirement beginning with the first month you are age 62 throughout the month.

✏**NOTE:** Unless you were born on the first or second day of the month, your first month of entitlement will be the month after your 62nd birthday.

For Social Security purposes, you attain your age the day before your birthday, so even if you were born on the second day of a month, you are considered to be age 62 as of the day before, and therefore age 62 throughout that month.

If you should become totally disabled before that, you may collect a Social Security disability benefit after five full months of disability. However, the disability benefit is payable only if you are totally disabled and your disability is expected to last for at least one year.

Q My husband is 66. He is presently working full time and this year had income of $100,000. Most likely his income will be similar next year. He plans to retire in three or four years. My question is: can he collect Social Security at this time while he is presently working and continue to earn income at this level?

A Yes, because your husband is over full retirement age. His earnings have no effect on his benefit amount. So even though he is earning a substantial sum of money, he can still receive his full Social Security benefits without reduction.

You also may receive benefits as his wife, if you are at least age 62, although if you have earnings, they may affect the payment of your benefits. But in any event, he should apply for benefits immediately because there are limits to the retroactivity of an application. For persons of full retirement age, the application can be *no more than six months retroactive*.

Q I will reach full retirement age on October 7. When should I apply for Social Security? I live in Greece.

A You should apply immediately because you may be eligible for benefits even though you are not yet of full retirement age. If your total earnings for 2007 for months before you turn full retirement age are less than $34,440, you may receive benefits for every month this year. However, you may not be able to receive benefits for months before your month of application. I would suggest that you file a *protective filing statement* immediately. You may file your application or a protective filing statement at any U.S. Foreign Service Post in Greece.

Q I am going to retire soon and I want to know how much I can earn a year in addition to my Social Security checks.

A It depends on how old you are. If you are over *Full Retirement Age*, then your earnings will have no effect on your benefits and you can earn as much as you like. For the year you attain *Full Retirement Age*, only the earnings in the months prior to the month of *Full Retirement Age* will count. For 2007, your exempt amount is $34,440. If the earnings for those months are less, then you will be entitled to full Social Security benefits for all months. If the earnings are over that amount, you will lose $1 in Social Security benefits for every $3 over that limit. If you will not reach *Full Retirement Age* this year, then the lower annual exempt amount figure applies.

For 2007, it is $12,960 per year, and you will lose $1 in benefits for every $2 in earnings above the limit (not $3 like it is for those of *Full Retirement Age*).

Q **I have filed for Social Security, which will begin in June. I will continue working and I need to know how much I can earn and how it is figured for the self-employed person. I make gross earnings of between $20,000 and $30,000, but not nearly as much after my expenses. Can you tell me how to figure what I can earn other than by using my tax returns? Will claiming my business expenses this year make it better or worse?**

A Social Security rules for earnings differ depending on whether you reach *Full Retirement Age* this year or not. If you do reach *Full Retirement Age* this year (2007), then you are allowed to earn up to $34,440 and it will have no effect at all on your Social Security benefits. If you do not reach *Full Retirement Age*, then you are allowed to earn only $12,960 per year before it will affect your benefits. If you earn over this annual exempt amount, then you will lose $1 for every $2 over the limit if you do not reach *Full Retirement Age* this year. If you are of *Full Retirement Age*, then you lose $1 for every $3 over the $34,440 limit.

☞**NOTE:** Only the earnings for months before you reach Full Retirement Age are counted.

Full Retirement Age used to be age 65. For those born after 1937, *Full Retirement Age* is gradually increasing in increments. For those born between 1938 and 1942, each year the age goes up in two month increments to 65 and two months, 65 and four months, etc. For those born from 1943 to 1954, it is age 66. It starts rising again for those born later, and eventually gets up to age 67. In your case, because you say that you will be beginning your Social Security benefits in June, I am assuming that you will be age 62 at that time. Your annual earnings for the year are the earnings that are used to calculate the deductions from your benefits—both your earnings *before and after* retirement.

Because you are self-employed, there are some special considerations you must take into account. First of all, Social Security generally will not take your word for it regarding the amount of your earnings, because you are in a position to control what is reported. They will want a complete explanation of why your earnings are less than they previously were. They will want to know if you have given up business, or if you hired new people to take over your duties. They will want to know specifically what you do, both before and after your retirement. It is very important to prepare carefully for that first interview.

You should be deducting your expenses from your gross income in order to calculate your net. Income taxes are payable only on net income. Social Security will use your tax returns as a starting point for determining your net earnings from self-employment, but they are not bound by the figures you report. If the figures do not make sense in light of the circumstances of your business, then they can determine that your earnings are too high to permit payment of any benefits.

I would suggest that you get your financial papers in order, including your tax returns with the proper deductions, and that you get prepared to verify every statement you make to Social Security regarding your customers, hours, duties, income, and expenses. Social Security in some cases actually will send someone to your business to verify any statements that you make.

For Example:
If you say that you will not be working three days a week, they will want to know what days you are not working and they will send someone there to look for themselves to see if they find you there. If they find any reason to doubt any of your statements, they can assume that your whole claim is false and not pay you anything, so it is important to be prepared for verification.

Q I am 63 and plan on retiring as of August first of this year (2007). As of August, I will have earned approximately $50,000 for this year. Will I be eligible for any benefits?

A You will be eligible for benefits beginning with August if your monthly earnings for August and each month thereafter are less than $1,080 per month. These are called *non-service months* and under the Social Security law, you are entitled to one year (called a *grace year*), in which you may use non-service months. Under the non-service month provision, you may receive a monthly benefit for each such month despite your annual earnings for that year. In your case, you will be over age 62 during this year and accordingly you will be able to receive Social Security retirement benefits.

It is important, however, that you go to your Social Security office before August, as your application for retirement benefits will have a limited *retroactive* effect because your benefits will be reduced for age. Accordingly, if you wait until September or October to file, you may *lose* several months' benefits.

Warning

The general rule of thumb would apply in your case: apply at least three months prior to your expected retirement date.

I would caution you, however, that since your retirement date is August 1, certain payments you receive in connection with your retirement may be counted as wages for the *earnings test* as of August, and therefore disqualify you for a monthly payment for August.

If you will be expecting to receive any lump sum payments at the time you retire, you may want to consider making your retirement date effective July 31 so as to avoid any question about entitlement for the month of August. If you cannot change the retirement date, then you want to look carefully at any payments you may be receiving at the time of your retirement. Some payments that are reported and are taxable as Social Security wages do not count for the earnings test used for the purposes of determining Social Security benefits. Such types of payments include certain lump sum retirement benefits, accumulated sick leave under a sick pay plan, deferred payment for work previously performed, and so forth.

Q **I will be 63 in August. How can I find out what my benefit would be if I sign up for Social Security on my next birthday? Thank you.**

A It is not wise to wait until your birthday to apply for Social Security, especially when you are already over age 62. That is because the application for Social Security benefits, if you are under *Full Retirement Age*, is not effective for *retroactive* benefits. If your Social Security earnings for the year 2007 are $12,960 or less, then your earnings will have no effect at all on your Social Security benefits and you could be eligible for monthly benefits beginning with January. However, if you do not apply for these benefits until August, you will lose seven months' worth of benefits because your application would have no retroactivity. Even if you earn over $12,960, you lose only $1 Social Security benefits for every $2 of excess wages.

For Example:
If you earned $21,680 for the year, then your earnings would be $8,720 over the limit. This would require the withholding of $4,360 of Social Security benefits. If your monthly benefit is $874 then you would be potentially

eligible for $6,118 in benefits for the months of January through July, but only $4,360 would have to be withheld based on your earnings. This would leave benefits payable to you for that period of $1,758.

In order to take advantage of that, however, your effective filing date would have to be January so as to maximize the number of months for which benefits could be paid. If you do not apply until August, you will lose all that money. Accordingly, the best thing to do when you are over 62 as of any January, is to file a *protective filing statement* with your local Social Security office.

This protective filing statement will secure your filing date. At the same time, you can request a benefit estimate. If it turns out that your earnings for the year will be less than the limit, or even over the limit that is allowed for the payment of benefits, then you will be protected. In order to make this work to your maximum advantage, you must have a January month of entitlement. When you file a protective filing statement, you do not have to file an application, but the statement will protect your filing date in case you file an application later.

In your case, I would suggest you immediately call your Social Security office to ask them to protect your filing date, and at the same time request a benefit estimate. Do not delay until your birthday. Do this now. Even if you cannot maximize your benefits for the year because you may have missed January filing, you may still be able to pick up some benefits if you act quickly.

Q I am 67 years old. I took $51,000 out of my IRA to pay for my condo. I have not worked since June of 2005. How come an article that was in the paper says I don't have to pay tax on any of my Social Security because of a law passed in 2000 that if you are between the age of 65 and 67, it is the same as if you are 70, and you can make as much as you want and not have your Social Security taxed? Who is right? Last year I had to pay taxes on $5,000-plus of my Social Security. What is the real law? I would love a comment from you. Thanks.

A You are mixing apples and oranges. The provision that you are referring to has to do with work deductions from Social Security benefits, not the taxation of Social Security benefits. Here's the way it works. The so-called *retirement test* is a provision that requires a Social Security beneficiary to lose benefits if earnings for the year exceed a certain annual limit.

The earnings for the year depend on your age. The amount of benefits you lose for excess earnings *also* depends on your age. At one time it was very simple. You would lose $1 in benefits for every $2 over the annual exempt amount. Over the years it has become much more complicated. Different annually exempt amounts were set for persons who were 65 and older and people who were under 65. Then the law provided that persons over 72 (reduced to age 70, and now changed to full retirement age) can earn as much as they like and have no loss of Social Security benefits. That is the law that was passed in the year 2000—the change to full retirement age for the exemption from the earnings test.

Under the law as it stands now, if you are over *Full Retirement Age*, then your earnings will have no effect on your Social Security benefits. However, if you receive income that is otherwise taxable, then you may have to pay tax on that income even if it is not considered *wages* for Social Security purposes. Additionally, if your total income, including otherwise non-taxable income such as Social Security benefits (but only a portion—50% to 85%) and municipal bond dividends, exceeds certain limits, you may have to pay taxes on your Social Security benefits.

In your case, because you are 67 years old, your annual earnings will have no effect on your entitlement to Social Security benefits. There will be no deductions from those monthly benefits no matter how much you earn per year.

For Example:
If your total income for an individual is between $25,000 and $34,000, then 50% of your Social Security benefits are taxable. If your income is over $34,000, up to 85% of your benefits are subject to taxation.

✐**NOTE:** This is income taxation payable to the Internal Revenue Service and not a deduction from your Social Security benefits.

The IRA distribution that you took should have no effect on your Social Security benefits and indeed should not even be subject to the Social Security tax on wages. However, it is income to you for IRS purposes. This may result in a portion of your Social Security benefits being taxed by the IRS as well.

Q I will be 62 in September and plan to take an early retirement at that time. If I continue to work parttime, I realize I am allowed to make $12,960 in 2007 without being penalized. If I go over, how and when will money be taken away? Do they withhold checks at the beginning of the year or after I hit my quota? Thank you for any help.

A Your first month of entitlement will be October unless you were born on September 1st or September 2nd. There is a requirement now that you must be 62 "throughout the month" in order to qualify for a retirement benefit. Your earnings for the entire year will be considered. The excess over the exempt amount will offset your Social Security benefits payable, at the rate of a loss of $1 in Social Security benefits for every $2 of wages over the limit.

For Example:

If you earn $2,000 over the limit, you will lose $1,000 in Social Security benefits. However, you may be eligible for a *grace year*. This is one year during which you may receive benefits in months where your earnings are less than $1,080 (for the year 2007—this will increase in future years). If your earnings for October, November, and December are less than this limit, then you will be able to receive your Social Security benefits despite your annual earnings. If you have earnings over that limit, then those months will be subject to withholding.

The *withholding* of benefits usually begins with the first month for which benefits are payable. The whole month will be withheld. Each following month's benefits will be withheld until the amount needed is satisfied. There is a possibility in very limited circumstances for the withholding to be prorated over the year's benefits rather than withheld all at once in the beginning. In your case, your earnings for the year before you turn 62 will also be included in calculating how much of your benefits must be withheld.

Q I returned to work part time after a number of years raising my kids. My last position was a substitute teacher. I was diagnosed with breast cancer and went through chemo, a mastectomy, more chemo, then radiation. I also have five children at home and was not able to continue to work. My question is: do I have the right to collect Social Security even though I was a part-time worker?

A As long as you have at least *40 quarters* of covered employment, you will be eligible for a Social Security retirement benefit at age 62. If you are totally disabled, you may also be eligible for a disability benefit, but your work history must be such that you have *20 quarters* of coverage within the 40 calendar quarters immediately preceding the onset of your disability. It does not matter that you may have been a part-time worker, although the amount of your benefit will be affected by the amount of your earnings. As long as you have the required number of quarters, you will be eligible for at least some benefit.

Q I am 63 years old, and I am thinking of retirement, but I am concerned. If I wanted to retire September 1, 2007, and I am currently working earning $3,000 per month, would this count against my earnings for the year 2007?

A Yes. Your entire year's earnings count for the *earnings test requirement*. However, if you do retire as of September 1 and your earnings for that month are less than $1,080, then you may receive a Social Security benefit for each month in which your earnings are less than that limit. You may only do this in one year (called the grace year).

Q If a person was born in March 1945, when do they receive their first Social Security benefit? When should a person born in 1945 start applying for Social Security?

A The first month of entitlement for a Social Security retirement benefit would be the first month you are age 62 throughout the month. If your birthday in March is not on the first or second day of the month, then you will not be entitled until April of the year you turn 62—in your case, 2007. You should go to the Social Security office three months before you turn 62 to file your application.

Q We were told that if you were over 70, your earnings will not be reduced by the Social Security benefits you receive. In other words, the Social Security received is not taxable and not added to the gross income.

A You are under several misconceptions. The law *used to be* that earnings after age 70 would not reduce Social Security benefits. It is now *Full Retirement Age,* which is increasing for those born after 1937. For those under *Full Retirement Age,* earnings affect the Social Security benefits, not the other way around. A beneficiary loses $1 of Social Security benefits for a portion of earnings in excess of the annual limit. The Social Security benefits, however, still may be subject to income tax if the *gross income* of the individual is over the applicable amount ($25,000 for an individual, $32,000 for a couple).

Q I will be turning 65 this year and I have two minor children, ages 12 and 16. Will my Social Security payments be increased because of having two minor children?

A Yes. You will receive benefits on behalf of your children because they are minors. The amount of each child's benefit will be 50% of your own primary insurance amount. Each child's benefit will be subject to a *family maximum* that will limit the total benefits payable on your account to approximately 150% to 175% of your primary insurance amount, depending on the amount of the benefits. The benefits you receive on behalf of the children are not payments for you, but must be used for the benefit of the children. If they are living with you, of course, you may apply these funds to the household expenditures.

Q My father-in-law worked for a few years; he stopped working in the 1980s. He is now 60 years old. Is he still entitled to Social Security for the years he worked?

A Probably not. He must have earned at least 40 quarters of coverage to qualify for his Social Security benefit. This would be ten years, although it does not have to be consecutive. It goes by calendar quarters. If he has 40 quarters, even though they may be spread out, he will be eligible. However, he would not be eligible until he turns 62.

Q When do I stop paying income tax on my Social Security? Is there a maximum age limit when I can earn as much as I want without paying income tax on my Social Security? Thanks.

A There is no age limit when you stop being liable for taxes on your benefits. The taxes are payable only if your income exceeds the applicable minimums, which vary depending on filing status and amount of income. You may be thinking of the earnings limits for retirement benefits. After you reach *Full Retirement Age*— previously age 65, but now increasing in two-months increments, your earnings will not cause your Social Security benefits to be reduced. You are always liable for taxes on Social Security income if over the applicable limits. You must pay Social Security tax and income tax on the wages.

Chapter 2

DISABILITY

This Social Security program is designed to replace income lost to a wage earner by reason of total disability. These benefits are not intended for temporary periods of disability. To qualify, the worker must be totally disabled from engaging in any employment even if it is not the worker's customary employment, and the disability must be expected to last for at least one year or to end in death. The age, education, and work experience of the worker is taken into account to determine if he or she could obtain work in a field other than his or her usual one.

The following questions discuss the details of this program, including the issues of the waiting period and unsuccessful work attempts, the definition of disability, and the interplay with other benefits.

Q **Where can I get information about disability benefits? I am already receiving Social Security. I am 66. I have a very debilitating medical condition. Thank you.**

A You cannot collect disability benefits because the amount of the disability benefit is the same as if you are full retirement age. In other words, the disability benefit is equal to the full-unreduced retirement benefit as if you had reached full retirement age in the year you became disabled. So even though you may be disabled, there is no additional benefit payable to you. If, however, your disability began earlier than the year you reached full retirement age, you may have some advantage in your benefit amount because of the way Social Security benefits are calculated.

You did not say when you became disabled, but if it was more than a few years ago, you may be able to derive some benefit. Additionally, Social Security disability benefits are not reduced for age, although there is a full five-month waiting period before the benefits become payable. An application for disability benefits can be *retroactive* for benefit payments for up to twelve months. However, if you were disabled even before that, the benefit payment can be recalculated based on the year of the onset of the disability, even if that is beyond the twelve-month retroactive period.

So my advice to you is to determine first of all when you became disabled. If it was before the year you reached full retirement age, then you may derive some benefit from filing for disability now. If it was in the year you attained full retirement age or later, then there would be no major advantage, unless the onset of the disability was more than six months before the month you reached full retirement age. If you receive retirement benefits before you reached full retirement age, they are reduced *actuarially*, depending on how young you are when you first begin the retirement benefits. There is no actuarial reduction for the disability benefits, so you can receive an unreduced benefit if it is based on disability for months before full retirement age.

Q **I retired at 49 with thirty years of service. I have been told that if I don't get a job within five years of my 62nd birthday, and something happens to me health-wise and I needed disability benefits, I wouldn't be entitled to them as I didn't work five years before I turned 62. Is this true?**

A The five-year requirement applies to the time you become disabled; not necessarily the time you turn 62. In order to be eligible for Social Security disability benefits, there is a recent work requirement.

In addition to having the required number of quarters that may be earned anytime throughout your work life, you must additionally have worked during twenty calendar quarters within the forty calendar quarters that immediately proceeded the onset of your disability. This is the so-called *20/40 Rule*. It may also be expressed as the *5 Year Rule* because twenty quarters comes to five years. The "five year" name is somewhat misleading because the years do not need to be consecutive. It goes by the quarters, which can be spread out, but it must be twenty quarters within the 40-quarter period prior to the onset of your disability.

Another way to look at that is that you will be covered for Social Security benefits for five years after you last work steadily. In your case, because you worked steadily up to age 49, you are covered for Social Security disability purposes until age 54. If you become disabled after that, you may not be eligible for Social Security disability. If, however, you work, even on a part-time basis and have covered employment for the continuing quarters, then your eligibility for disability benefits will continue. To get a Social Security credit for a quarter, you must earn $870 for each quarter.

Q **My question is why is it so hard to get your benefits for disability? I have been off work for over a year and I am still not sure how to get an answer. I was denied once, but I asked for a review and I never got an answer. I called and they said they never received the papers.**

What is a disability? I cannot do my normal job. I may never be able to do labor work. If you can explain to me what I can do, I will be grateful. Thank you.

A The requirement for disability under Social Security is very strict. You must be totally and permanently disabled from performing *any* substantial gainful activity. This means that even if you cannot do your regular job, you are not considered disabled if you can do some other work. When Social Security evaluates your ability to do other work, they will look first at your physical abilities to determine what type of tasks you can perform. Then they will look at your age, your education, and your work experience to determine whether or not you have any skills that you can transfer into a new line of work considering what your remaining physical abilities are.

Because they are so strict, most claims for disability benefits are denied on the first application. However, it is very important for you to continue on the appeals process, as many times these denials are reversed.

The first level of review after the initial denial is *reconsideration* and that is basically a paperwork review. You have sixty days from the date of the denial in which to request reconsideration. In your case, Social Security says they never received the papers, so I would suggest that you go down to the office and ask to file a late request for reconsideration. They may accept a late request if *good cause* is shown for the delay. If they do not, then you should refile your disability application and request reconsideration if it is denied again.

After the reconsideration, you are entitled to a hearing before an administrative law judge. That is your best chance of reversing the denial because you will be able to appear in person to present evidence and to have an attorney appear with you.

Warning

It is very important that you *do* obtain an attorney to represent you, especially at this hearing level.

Most attorneys who handle Social Security claims will accept your case on a *contingency* basis. This means that you will not have to pay any attorney's fee unless you win. If you do win, Social Security will withhold 25% of your past-due benefits pending approval of an attorney's fee. Social Security Administration must approve the fee arrangement.

To obtain an attorney qualified to handle a Social Security claim I would suggest you contact the National Organization of Social Security Claimants' Representatives. The number is 800-431-2804. This organization should be able to steer you in the right direction to obtain a competent attorney. Good luck.

Q I started receiving disability checks when I was 57. I am now 60. When I turn 62, do I have to do anything to continue getting my disability check or do I just get a regular check after 62 and not disability? Will the amount of my check change at 62 or 65? Thanks for your time.

A You do not have to do anything. The Social Security disability check will continue until you attain full retirement age. At that time, it will be converted automatically into an unreduced retirement benefit. The amount of the check will stay the same.

Q I have self-paid disability insurance that I am now collecting at age 58. They will pay me until I am 65. I need to apply for Social Security disability now, but I am concerned that Social Security will not pay if I am collecting from a private insurance company and pay no taxes on this money. Will Social Security pay disability if I am approved without a penalty due to the other insurance?

A Absolutely yes. Any other income, pensions or benefits that you receive, except for workers' compensation, will have no effect on Social Security disability benefits. It is only the workers' compensation benefits that are offset from the Social Security disability. Your private disability insurance will have no effect whatsoever.

Q I do want to change my direct deposit to a different bank. Do I need a form for this change? Please advise if I should go to a Social Security office for this change. Thank you.

A The easiest way is to go to the new bank and tell them that you want the benefits changed. They have all the forms and will be glad to do whatever paper work is necessary to have your money deposited into their bank. Alternatively, you may go to the Social Security office to request the appropriate forms, but I recommend dealing with the bank.

Q My husband is having surgery to replace joints in his feet due to arthritis. He is only 46 and does not collect any benefits, but he will be out of work for some time. Is there any way for him to collect from Social Security while he is off temporarily?

A Social Security disability is designed for permanent and total disability cases. This means that the condition must be expected to last for at least one year. If his condition is expected to improve within twelve months, then he will not be eligible for Social Security disability.

Q How much are you allowed to make when you receive Social Security disability each month? I receive another disability payment from where I work and in May I will receive 60% of my wages. My Social Security starts in June. What is the

limit on the amount you are allowed to receive besides Social Security payments? Also, what can you tell me about medical assistance? I don't have any. Thank you.

A The only unearned income that affects your Social Security disability is workers' compensation benefits. The payments you receive from a long-term disability plan or a company disability plan will have no effect on your Social Security disability benefits. You will be entitled to Medicare coverage after twenty-four months of entitlement to Social Security disability benefits.

Q **I am on disability and would like to know how much money I can make a month without jeopardizing my Social Security check.**

A For the year 2007, you can earn on average no more than $900 per month ($1,500 if you are blind). If your earnings over a period of time average less than this sum, your earnings will not be considered to be substantial gainful activity. Such earnings will have no effect on your continued entitlement to Social Security benefits.

✎**NOTE**: This amount will increase in future years. The amounts of the increases are not yet determined, but they are published each year by Social Security. You may visit my website at **www.socialsecuritybenefitshandbook.com** for the most recent information.

Q My brother has been collecting Social Security disability for the last three years. He and his wife are finally getting a divorce and he is trying to get $400 a month from her. Will that affect the amount he receives from Social Security disability?

A No. Unearned income (other than workers' compensation benefits) has no effect on Social Security disability benefits.

Q I sure hope that you can help me. I am writing on behalf of my very ill mother. Almost three years ago she was diagnosed with fibromyalgia and a degenerative joint disease. She also had a heart attack around that time. She has not been able to work for the past three years due to the severe pain of the fibromyalgia and degenerative joint disease. She has applied for disability benefits only to be turned down again and again. In November she was diagnosed with breast cancer. She, of course, had surgery and they found that eight of twelve lymph nodes were also cancerous. She reapplied for her disability benefits and yet again has been denied. I don't understand this.

She goes for chemotherapy twice a month and has to do this for the next six months. At her first chemotherapy treatment, the oncologist also diagnosed her with diabetes. After they are finished with that, she has to go through more months of radiation every day. The panel states that they still think that she is able to work. I have seen my mother in severe pain on a daily basis. Some days it is all she can do to get herself out of bed.

This panel of doctors has never seen my mother and the pain that she is in. She is ready to just give up. She lives on absolutely no income. She relies on family members to make sure that she gets her utilities and such paid. We had contacted a lawyer in the past and he told her that if she didn't have knee surgery she would never get it. Well who is supposed to pay for that? This is, of course, before the cancer and diabetes diagnosis. Please, please any information that would help would be greatly appreciated. We are so very desperate at this point.

A Sadly, Social Security is very strict on making determinations of disability. It is very important for you to retain an attorney who has experience with Social Security disability claims. Do not give up. Frequently, cases are won at a hearing where your mother is entitled to appear in person and witnesses may testify on her behalf. She is entitled to be represented by an attorney at that point.

I would suggest that you contact the National Organization of Social Security Claimant's Representatives, which is a lawyers association of attorneys who specialize in Social Security. They have a toll-free number during Eastern timezone business hours. You may reach them at 800-431-2804 and they will refer you to an experienced Social Security attorney in your area. Best wishes for your mom.

Q My sister suffered a stroke in October. She is paralyzed on her right side and is unable to speak. She is 57 years old and married. Can she draw Social Security benefits due to her disability?

A She can only get disability benefits if she has the sufficient amount of work on her own account. In addition to being fully insured (having forty quarters of coverage), she also must have worked in at least twenty calendar quarters out of the last forty calendar quarters before the onset of her disability. If she does not meet this work requirement, then she cannot collect any Social Security benefits unless she is a widow. In that event, she could collect disabled widows' benefits because she is over 50 years old. Otherwise, she will have to wait until she is 62 to collect as a wife on her husband's account.

Q **I was injured and am not able to return to full-time employment. Is there any full or partial disability available under these circumstances?**

A Social Security does not provide for any partial disability, but it does provide disability benefits for workers who are totally and permanently disabled. *Totally disabled* means unable to perform *any* kind of work activity, considering your age, education, and work experience. You may be disqualified for disability benefits even if you can't perform your regular job, if there is other work that you could perform.

Additionally, the disability must be considered to be *permanent*. This means that it must be expected to last for at least twelve months or to result in death. On top of that, there is a waiting period before any disability benefits are payable. No benefits are payable during the first five full months of disability, even if you are otherwise entitled. In your case, September would not count as a month because it is not a full month of disability. I would recommend that you contact your local Social Security office to file a disability application if you feel you meet these requirements.

Q **Can a Social Security Disability (SSD) recipient become a board member of a not-for-profit organization without losing benefits? No salary would be received for this position and it is a way of doing something worth living for instead of doing nothing at all. Please advise. Thank you.**

A Yes, you can. SSD (Social Security Disability) is payable so long as you are unable to perform *substantial gainful activity*. Under the rules, earnings less than $900 per month ($1,500 if you are blind) are not considered substantial, and therefore have no effect on your disability entitlement. However, if your activity is worth more than this amount per month, even though you are not being paid, Social Security could determine that you are not disabled because you are capable of working. You do not have to report to them how you spend your time if you are not being paid. This would only come up if Social Security were to review your continuing eligibility.

Q **My father collects Social Security. He was just declared legally blind. Do his benefits increase? Thanks.**

A Sorry to hear about your dad. If he is under full retirement age, he can apply for disability benefits on the basis of the blindness. His benefits will be recalculated and paid on an unreduced basis. If he is over full retirement age, the benefits would be no higher. Disability benefits are available only under full retirement age.

Q **I need to apply for Social Security Disability benefits. Can you tell me what I need to do, and whether I can do it via phone or on the Internet?**

A You can now apply for disability benefits online, by going to **www.ssa.gov**. Some district offices may make arrangements for telephone interviews. Gather together and have available the names and addresses of all your treating doctors. You should also include the names and addresses of all hospitals and facilities where tests were done. You should be prepared with the dates you last worked; when you were hospitalized; when tests were done; and, when you saw each doctor.

They will ask you about your past work experience, education, and your current physical activities. They want very detailed answers to get a picture of your functional capacity, the physical requirements of your occupation, and your ability to transfer job skills to other occupations if you can no longer do your regular job. You should have your last year's W-2 and birth certificate. If you receive workers' compensation, you will have to provide them with that information as well.

Q My husband has been diagnosed with Alzheimer's. Is this considered a disability? He is 69 years old. If it is a disability, can he receive additional income?

A Sorry to hear about your husband's health problems. Unfortunately, disability benefits are not paid beyond age 65, even if the person is disabled.

Q My doctor has made me quit work and told me to apply for my disability benefits. I have a small 401(k) plan and I need to know if that would interfere with being able to qualify. I have been told that it would. My husband also has a small 401(k) plan.

A Your assets such as savings and 401(k)s have no effect on your entitlement to Social Security benefits (SSI is different) because this is a social insurance program based on your *contributions* (payroll taxes) to the system. If you meet the *insured status* requirements for disability, and are *totally disabled*, you may be eligible. You should definitely follow your doctor's orders and apply.

If you are turned down on the first application, do not give up, because you have the right to a reconsideration and then a hearing. Frequently, claims that are denied at the first application and reconsideration are approved after a hearing where you attend before a judge in person with an attorney. Attorneys who take Social Security cases generally accept *contingency* fees, which means you pay them only if you win.

There are asset limitations for SSI (Supplemental Security Income) payments, which are a federally funded welfare program for the disabled, blind, and elderly. This program is also administered by the Social Security Administration. Many people get confused because regular Social Security disability benefits are referred to as SSDI (Social Security Disability Insurance).

Q **My husband has not been able to work for quite some time, due to a rare, chronic disease. He is 42 years old. In August 1999, he began the long process of applying for disability benefits. On December 18, he received a letter from Social Security denying him benefits. He is now in the process of filing a *reconsideration*. Today he got a phone call from his place of work stating if he does not come back to work by February, he will be terminated. They do not have to hold his job for him any longer than twelve months. Since he is very sick, but has a family to support, he will be FORCED back to work. Will the *reconsideration* continue even if he is forced back to work? I would appreciate any help you can give me.**

A Yes. Keep going. Many cases are won at later appeal stages. The return to work may prove unsuccessful. It may be disregarded by Social Security if it lasts no more than three months, sometimes longer in certain situations. He may also be entitled to nine months of a trial work period.

Q I am collecting Social Security disability because of multiple sclerosis. I've been offered a part-time job, but need to know how much money I can make without losing my Social Security disability.

A Earnings as an employee averaging over $900 a month ($1,500 if you are blind) will ordinarily demonstrate that an individual is engaged in substantial gainful activity, and that benefits should stop. If you earn under this average monthly amount, your earnings will not affect your continuing entitlement.

Q My friend filed a disability claim about three months ago. He has not received an answer as to whether he was approved or denied. Is there a certain amount of time that Social Security has to give an answer?

A It usually takes at least three months. Disability claims are often denied the first time, but then are won on appeal. Get a lawyer if you are denied the first time.

✑**NOTE**: Even if you are denied, request a *reconsideration* and then a *hearing* if necessary.

Q My wife and I have a question with which you may be able to help. My wife has had two individual mastectomies four years apart. After the last procedure, she has been in constant pain and is seeing a psychologist on a regular basis to help her deal with the emotional and physical pain. She was granted Social Security disability benefits in October 1998, *retroactive* to April. We used the services of an attorney that specializes in this area. She was informed at that time that her case would be reviewed in the future. She is in constant pain due to lymphodema and cannot drive for more than thirty minutes at a time nor lift anything more than five lbs. She is 57 years old, a registered nurse, and wondering if her review will continue her benefits.

I guess my questions to you are the following: Should we employ an attorney for the review if it is denied and what do you think her chances are for continuation of benefits? Does she have a right of appeal if denied? Do her benefits continue while the appeal process is being reviewed? Any suggestions you may have would be very much appreciated.

A Your wife's benefits will not likely be cut off unless she has regained a capacity to work in substantial gainful employment. From the way you have described her physical capacity, it does not appear she can work. I would never tell you not to retain an attorney, but I will tell you to make sure the one you retain has significant expertise in *this area* of law.

If the decision is made to stop her benefits, you have the right to a *reconsideration*, and a *hearing* before an administrative law judge, as well as further appeals to the Appeals Council, and then review by a federal court. If you are cutoff, you may request that benefits continue pending the outcome of the appeal, but this continuation only goes through the hearing level.

Warning

You must request the continuation of benefits within ten days after the termination notice!

If you ultimately lose on appeal, you may have to repay the money, but may also be eligible for a waiver of the overpayment.

Q **I am receiving a Social Security disability check of $1,015 a month. If I do want to go back to work, do I lose my disability check every month?**

A If you are able to perform *substantial gainful activity*, your disability benefits may be terminated, but not right away. The first question is whether or not you will be performing *substantial gainful activity*. Under the Social Security regulations, this means earnings greater than $900 per month on average during a work period. That figure is applicable for the year 2002, but will be rising in future years. If you are a blind individual, then that figure is $1,500 per month.

Generally, when a disability beneficiary attempts to return to work, he or she is granted a *trial work period*. A trial work period is the time during which your earnings will not be used to terminate your entitlement to disability benefits. You can work during nine months before Social Security will consider terminating your disability. If your attempt to work is unsuccessful, your benefits will continue. A trial work period is any month in which you have earnings greater than $640 per month in 2007.

Warning

After the end of a trial work period, Social Security will determine if you are performing substantial gainful activity. If so, your benefits will be terminated three months after the month Social Security determines that you are no longer disabled.

Q **There is a young man I know who gets disability for what he said is a back injury. He works for cash every day. He has a lawn and landscaping business and there is nothing wrong with him. He just wants to live off everyone else. I am young and think it's not fair! How do I go about reporting him? What information do I need to do it? Thank you for your time.**

A It is very discouraging to see people trying to cheat the system, if in fact that is the case. Social Security does permit disability beneficiaries to attempt to work. If their earnings are below certain levels, they may continue to receive their disability benefits even though the work activity may continue. However, it is also true that many people do try to cheat the system by not reporting their earnings to Social Security and sometimes even to the Internal Revenue Service.

You can report this individual to the Social Security Administration. They have local offices throughout the country and you may do this in person or by telephone. The Social Security toll-free number is 800-772-1213. You may also locate your Social Security office by looking in the blue pages of your telephone book under "U.S. Government." You may also ask at your post office where the local Social Security office is located.

If you do report this individual, you should have his full name and address. If you believe he is working in a business, any information you can provide to Social Security will be verified. If you give the name of the business or some of his customers, they will be able to contact them to determine if he is legitimate or if he is cheating.

Q My son was in an accident and suffered a brain injury. Currently, he receives Social Security disability. In October, he started working at our local library in a clerical capacity. He had a job coach through the Office of Vocational Rehabilitation. He made over the allowed $900 about five months out of the nine-month trial work period. His job coach was with him during this period and trained him. He can only learn new tasks through constant repetition, which is how he learned his job.

Once the job coach cut her hours, my son's hours were decreased because he was not able either mentally or physically to perform his job. His stamina is low and he has trouble concentrating and focusing. He has difficulty learning anything new. He is unable to retain new information and he has short-term memory loss. The last nine months he has averaged about $700 per month. Now Social Security wants

to discontinue his payments because of the trial work period. We live in Pennsylvania. Any advice you can give would be appreciated. Thank you.

A The monthly amount for determining *substantial gainful activity*: for the year 2007 it is $900 per month. (The amount rises each year.) If your son is earning below those levels, he will not be considered to be performing substantial gainful activity and his benefits may be resumed. If he is earning above these higher levels, then you should try to determine what portion of his pay is actually *subsidized* by special job considerations given to him by his employer. You mentioned that he has been unable to do his job without the job coach, so obviously there is some element here of special consideration given to him if he is continuing to work.

Social Security has the authority to determine the actual earning figure based on the *value* of his services, rather than the actual paycheck itself if there is a situation where an employer is giving special consideration to a handicapped worker. If you can establish that he is not fully earning his pay and if you can also establish that the value of his pay after you extract out the subsidy element is less than the substantial gainful activity limits, then he may continue to work and receive the Social Security disability. If you attempt this and it is determined that he is performing substantial gainful activity anyway, you should file a request for a *reconsideration*. If that is unsuccessful, you should request a *hearing* before an administrative law judge.

Many times determinations made at the lower levels are reversed by hearing officers. At a *hearing* you are able to appear with your son. He is able to testify. The job coach can testify or someone from the employer can testify as well. Best wishes.

Q I applied for Social Security disability and was turned down. I applied for reconsideration and was turned down again. I am now going to a hearing, which won't be for some time, but what are my chances going in front of a judge?

A Your chances are very good of winning your disability benefits in front of a judge. The vast majority of disability applications are turned down at the initial application level, as well as at the reconsideration level. However, significant numbers are granted at the hearing. You will be entitled to be represented by an attorney at that time and I would suggest that you retain one. You may call the National Organization of Social Security Claimant's Representatives at a toll-free number to find an attorney who specializes in Social Security disability cases. The toll-free number is 800-431-2804 and they are open during Eastern time zone business hours.

Q I am a teacher and my doctor says I shouldn't be working because of an illness. He said I can collect disability. My question: Am I entitled to disability as a teacher in a public school system? Thank you for your kind consideration.

A If your employment is covered by Social Security, you may be eligible for disability benefits if you meet the work and medical requirements. Not all public employees are covered by Social Security. If you have FICA deductions from your paycheck, you are in the regular Social Security system. If your employment is not covered by Social Security, your public employment benefits most likely will provide a disability pension.

Q I filed an appeal with the Social Security Administration over two years ago and I have heard nothing. When I call, they tell me that someone will review my case. I need help. I am disabled and the stress is not good for my current condition, which has worsened since my consult with the Social Security doctors. Can someone out there please help or provide me with a name and number for someone who can?

A At this point I would suggest you contact your U.S. senator or congressperson to ask him or her to check into this for you. This is way too long for an appeal's decision. Many times an elected federal official can help your case get the attention it needs for a final resolution. Although the intervention of your congressperson or senator will not affect the merits of the decision it will certainly take it out of whatever pile it is in and put it on a front burner. You should contact your U.S. senator or congressperson immediately to ask for his or her help.

Q I am receiving Social Security disability benefits. A friend and I went to the casino and I won $2,000. How do I pay taxes on that? I didn't have them take out taxes at the time. What about my Social Security benefits? Does this money affect my benefits?

A Your casino winnings will have no effect on your Social Security benefits. You may not owe any taxes on the winnings if your total taxable income is below the threshold set by tax law. I would suggest you consult with an accountant or you can call the IRS to get further information.

Chapter 3

SURVIVOR BENEFITS

In this section, we deal with one of the most important Social Security programs—benefits payable to survivors of deceased workers. Generally speaking, a widow is entitled to receive benefits on her deceased spouse's account beginning at age 60, or as early as age 50 in the event of total disability. The amount of the benefit is reduced to 71½% at age 60 or earlier (in the event of disability).

Unlike wives' or husbands' benefits, a widow or widower may collect benefits on the deceased spouse's account and then switch over to his or her own account if he or she has earnings on his or her own earnings record. In this way, the widow or widower can collect an unreduced benefit at full retirement age on one account or the other.

A surviving, divorced wife who was married for at least ten years may also collect as a widow on a deceased ex-husband's account, and children, including stepchildren, of the worker may also collect up to age 18, or 19 if they are still in high school. College benefits for children have been eliminated.

In this chapter we will discuss questions as to the several different kinds of survivor benefits and the interplay with other benefits.

Q My 46-year-old, totally disabled spouse died in March. Am I entitled to any of his Social Security benefits? If so, how do I apply? If not, why?

A As a surviving spouse, you are entitled to receive a widow's benefit beginning at age 60, if you have not remarried before that age. The benefits are also payable at age 50 if you are totally disabled and unmarried before age 50. If you have young children under age 16 (or disabled) in your care, then you may be entitled to benefits as a young mother.

To apply for the benefits, I would suggest that you go to the Social Security office three months before your expected eligibility. In your case, if you have no young children and are not disabled, then your first eligibility would be at age 60.

Q Please tell me if you are a woman aged 58 and your spouse at 65 commits suicide, are you entitled to widow's pension if he was already drawing a pension? I have been told that I wouldn't be entitled till I turn 62. Is this true? Thanks for your help.

A It is not true. You can collect a widow's benefit beginning at age 60. If you are totally disabled, you may collect if you are at least 50 years old. It doesn't matter that your husband was already drawing from Social Security—that makes no difference.

Q I will be full retirement age on September 8, 2007. I had planned to sign up for my benefits in July. I am now wondering if I should sign up to start collecting my ex-husband's benefits. He is deceased. I intend to continue working at my full-time job as long as I am physically able to do so. My ex-husband and I were married for twelve years, so I know I qualify in that respect. I know his benefits will be lower than mine. Could I possibly collect his benefits until I reach full retirement age and then collect my own (not both at once, of course)? I have a 44-year-old son who has a mental disability and is unable to work. I am his sole support at this time and really need some extra income to pay some bills. I don't want to jeopardize my own benefits, which should be over $1,000 a month. I want to do the correct thing. Please advise my options.

A I would suggest that you get into the Social Security office immediately. Because you will reach full retirement age in 2007, only your earnings for the months of January through August will count toward the annual exempt amount. If that is less than $34,440, then you will be eligible to receive Social Security disability benefits for every month in 2007, provided you apply. You may apply for surviving divorced wife benefits on your husband's account and receive them on a reduced basis before you reach full retirement age. You can then switch over to your own account at full retirement age on an unreduced basis. It is important for you to know the exact amounts of benefits both on his account and on your account so that you can determine which way is more advantageous to you.

I would suggest that you go to the Social Security office immediately and file a *protective filing statement*. Request estimates of the benefits on both accounts so that you can compare your options. Unlike wives, widows have the option to collect benefits on one account and then switch over to the other at full retirement age. To take advantage of this, you must protect your filing date as soon as possible. If your child was disabled before age 22, he may be able to receive benefits on your account or on your ex-husband's account as a disabled adult child. You should explore that possibility as well.

Q **My children's father died in an accident when they were 5 and 7 years old. They have been receiving survivor's benefits. Now my son is a junior in high school and we are looking for colleges. I have heard that if they continue their education, they would still receive survivor's benefits and I have heard this no longer is true. Is there a continuing benefit or is there anything they can apply for to help them through college due to their father's death?**

A At one time Social Security survivor's benefits paid children's benefits through their college years up to the age of 22. This has been changed some time ago and now children are eligible to receive survivor benefits only while they are in high school or secondary school up to the age of 19, if a full-time student.

If a child is disabled before the age of 22, then he or she may continue to receive benefits as an adult disabled child. Unfortunately, Social Security has no provisions for surviving children while they are in college.

Q My husband passed away seventeen months ago at age 66. At that time, I sent the marriage certificate and received the death benefit of $255, if I remember the sum correctly. I have not remarried and will be 60 soon. Do I remember some benefits starting for widows at age 60 as long as there has not been a remarriage? If a monthly check is granted when I am 62, do I apply for my own, if larger, or how long can I collect this widow's monthly? Thanks.

A You do remember correctly—the lump sum death benefit is $255. You are eligible for widow's benefits at age 60. This benefit will be reduced because you are under *Full Retirement Age*. You will receive 71% of your husband's primary insurance amount. You may collect the widow's benefit for the rest of your life.

If you are also eligible for Social Security on your own account, you may switch over when you become eligible. The earliest you can be eligible for retirement benefits on your own account is age 62. You will have the option of taking your own at age 62 (if that would be higher) or wait until age 65 when you may take a full *unreduced* benefit on your own account, which may be even higher still. It is important that you get to the Social Security office to make your application for the widow's benefit before the month you turn 60 so that you do not lose any benefits.

Q My mother and father were separated when my father passed away. He was receiving Social Security disability benefits at the time of his death. Will my mother be able to

receive his Social Security retirement benefits and hers when she retires or will she receive the greater of the two? Or, will she just be eligible for hers?

A Your mother is the legal widow of your father and she will therefore be eligible for widow's benefits when she turns age 60. If benefits on her own account would be higher at age 62 or age 65, she may switch over at that time to her own account. However, she will not get double benefits.

Q **When my daughter's father passed away, would she have been notified if she was to receive his Social Security or could it be possible that she was notified through his ex-wife and my daughter was never informed?**

A I am a little confused by your question. I am not sure who you are referring to when you say "she was notified through his ex-wife." But in any event, it is possible that Social Security is unaware that your daughter is potentially eligible on her deceased father's account. Whoever notified Social Security of his death may not have informed them that he was the father of your daughter.

I would suggest that you contact Social Security yourself to determine if your daughter is eligible for benefits on her father's account. If she is under age 18 (or a full-time student in high school up to age 19) or is a disabled adult who has been disabled since before age 22, she may be eligible for benefits on her father's account. When you contact Social Security, it would be very helpful if you have the father's Social Security number. If not, his name, last known address, employer, date of birth, and date of death would enable them to locate his record.

Q **I was married to my ex-husband for ten years and two months. He passed away five years ago at age 53. We have been divorced for over twenty years. I have not remarried and he never remarried. I have worked for the past thirty years and am age 55 currently. At age 60, would I be eligible for the "aged widow" benefit from his Social Security and could I continue to work?**

A Because you were married for at least ten years before you were divorced, you will be eligible to receive an aged widow's benefit at age 60 on his account. However, your earnings at that time may affect the benefits if they exceed the annual exempt amount. If they do, then you will lose $1 in Social Security benefits for every $2 over the limit. I do not know what the limit will be in five years as it increases every year. The current limit for 2007 for persons under *Full Retirement Age* is $12,960 per year. You can earn over that limit and still receive some Social Security benefits, but you will lose $1 for every $2 over the limit.

It is important for you to protect your filing date as of the first month you turn age 60 so that you can maximize any possible benefits payable to you even if you have some earnings over the annual limit.

✎**NOTE:** As a widow, you can collect a reduced widow's benefit and then switch over to your own account at age 62 or full retirement age. The widow's benefit, of course, will be reduced, but the reduction of the widow's benefit will not cause any additional reduction in the benefit on your own account.

You could receive the reduced widow's benefit up until *Full Retirement Age* and then switch over to your own account on an unreduced basis when you reach *Full Retirement Age*.

✎**NOTE:** For you, because you were born in 1946, your *Full Retirement Age* is 66.

Q My dad passed away and he was collecting Social Security. Is there a death benefit?

A There is a $255 death payment, but it goes to the surviving spouse. If there is no spouse, then it goes to the children who are eligible for *survivor benefits* on his account. These benefits are paid to children under 18, or to adult disabled children. If there is no spouse or eligible children, no death benefit is payable.

Q Could you please explain to me a little bit about survivor benefits? Who is eligible to receive my Social Security benefits when I die? I didn't think anyone could claim them, but my wife has heard differently. A friend of hers told her that she was receiving a benefit from her deceased spouse! Is that possible? And what benefit amount of his Social Security is she eligible to receive? Thank you for your answer to this inquiry.

A Social Security provides *survivor benefits* to:

- aged widows;
- disabled widows;
- young mothers;
- surviving divorced wives; and,
- children.

To qualify as an aged widow, the surviving spouse must be at least 60 years old. The amount of the benefit at that age is 71½% of the worker's full benefit. If the widow receives the benefit beginning with *Full Retirement Age,* then she will receive 100% of the deceased's benefit. A *disabled widow* is entitled to receive benefits if she is at least 50 years old and totally disabled. The amount of her benefit is the same as if she were age 60.

☞**NOTE:** Widows' benefits are payable also to widowers.

Also, young mothers (and fathers) are entitled to receive widow's benefits if they are the surviving widow and have a child of the wage earner under age 16 (or disabled) in their care. These benefits end when the youngest child turns 16 but can resume when the widow becomes age 60 (or 50 if totally disabled).

Divorced wives who have been married at least ten years and are not remarried before age 60, can also receive a widow's benefit from their ex-spouse. Children can receive benefits until they are age 18, but if they are in high school, the benefits can continue until age 19. If a student turns 19 during the school year, the child can receive benefits till the end of the semester in which he or she turns 19. Also, benefits are payable to children who become totally disabled before age 22 for as long as the disability lasts.

Q**I am a social worker and one of my clients is disabled. That is not germane to my question, however. My client was married for eleven years to a person whom she divorced after the eleven years. He remarried and has since died. He supposedly committed suicide, although my client does not think this is the case. She had two children by this man and the children are receiving survivor benefits. Is their mother—my client—eligible for survivor benefits as well?**

A Yes, your client is entitled to mother's benefits as a surviving divorced mother if at least one of the children is under the age of 16 and in her care. There is no ten-year marriage requirement for entitlement to surviving divorced *mothers' benefits*, provided she has not remarried.

Q I am about to marry a man whose wife passed away three years ago. He has been collecting Social Security for their daughters ever since. He has postponed our wedding for fear that once we marry he will lose the Social Security benefits for his daughters. He does not collect any for himself as the spouse of the deceased. Will Social Security stop for his children once we are married? I have no plans to adopt his daughters.

A The children are entitled due to the fact of their relationship to the deceased worker and their age. They will continue to receive these survivor benefits until they turn 18 (or 19 if they are still in high school). The remarriage of their father will have no effect whatsoever on these benefits.

Q My husband passed away two years ago. He was 62 and he was collecting disability payments from Social Security. I am now 35 years old. I want to know if I am able to collect his Social Security. If so, what do I need to do?

A To qualify as a widow on your husband's account you must be either age 60, age 50 and totally disabled, or have a child of his under age 16 in your care. If you fall within any of these categories, then you should go to your Social Security office to apply for the benefits. You will need your marriage certificate, your birth certificate, and your children's birth certificates if they are minors.

Q After my husband of twenty years passed away, I remarried. I did not collect any Social Security benefits after my husband's death because I had a good-paying job. Then I remarried and after six years divorced. Am I eligible to receive widow's benefits if I discontinue my job?

A If you are age 60, you can collect widow's benefits on your first husband's account. Although you remarried, that marriage has been terminated, so at the time of your current application, you will be unmarried. Because you were not married at least ten years to the second husband, you will not be able to collect benefits on his account at age 60, however.

Q I would like to know if I am eligible to collect my husband's Social Security at age 60 because I am a widow? How soon do I have to apply? Am I able to collect at 60 and if I marry down the road, can I still receive that benefit?

A As long as your husband had enough quarters of coverage under Social Security, you will be able to collect as his widow when you turn age 60. If you are totally disabled, you may collect after age 50. You should apply for the benefit three months before your 60th birthday. Bring with you to the Social Security office your marriage certificate, your husband's death certificate, and your birth certificate.

A remarriage at age 60 or later will have no effect on your widow's benefits. If you remarry before age 60, you will not be entitled.

Q My mom recently passed away. She only worked four or five years in her life and was receiving spouse benefits. Does any of that money revert back to my father?

A No. Your mother received benefits on your father's work record. She did not qualify for benefits on her own account because she only had four or five years of work. Likewise, no survivor benefits are payable on her account.

Q My question is: I have been a widow for the past twenty-eight years. My husband was in the U.S. Air Force at the time of his demise. We were only married eighteen months before his drowning accident. I would like to know if I am eligible for spousal benefits at my retirement. I am 49 years of age now and am still unmarried.

A You will be potentially eligible for a widow's benefit on your husband's account. You may receive this benefit at age 60, or if you are totally disabled, beginning at age 50. If you are working in Social Security covered employment, you will also be eligible for benefits on your own account if you have the sufficient number of quarters. You may be able to collect the widow's benefit on a reduced basis and then switch over to your own benefit at a later date. You must be 62 to collect on your own account.

Q I am a 61-year-old single mom and grandma. My ex-husband died in November. He always told me that I would be able to collect his Social Security after he died. We were married for fifteen years.

I also wanted to ask this question (it is a strange one). Both of my parents are deceased. What happens to all of the Social Security dollars that they paid? Isn't that something that the children have a right to? Just curious, thanks.

A You are entitled at present to a surviving divorced wife's benefit under your ex-husband's account. You were married for over ten years and you are over age 60. You should contact the Social Security office immediately to apply for those benefits.

I am assuming you are not working. If you are working, then your earnings could have an effect on those benefits payable if your earnings are substantial. In any event, you should check with Social Security because it is possible to receive benefits even though your earnings may be high.

Your question about your parents' Social Security contributions is a good one. The monies your parents paid into the system have been spent long ago on current benefits. Social Security is not like a retirement account or an annuity. Rather, it is simply a transfer of income from workers to retirees, people with disabilities, and survivors. The taxes taken from your Social Security benefits are paid out at the same time as benefits to beneficiaries of Social Security. There are no rights to these taxes. Even though the law refers to these taxes as "contributions"; they are simply taxes.

Chapter 4   MEDICARE

Medicare is a health insurance program, which is not precisely a Social Security program because it is funded from separate taxes. These taxes are deducted from wage earners' paychecks along with the Social Security taxes. Social Security administers the Medicare program in terms of the eligibility for the coverage, but does not administer the payment of the medical benefits directly. Various contracting insurance companies around the country take care of that.

Medicare is generally available for workers and their dependents who are 65 years of age. It is also available for disabled workers who have been entitled to Social Security disability benefits for at least twenty-four months.

Medicare provides for the payment of in-patient hospital expenses after the first day and for 80% of physicians' expenses. It currently does not cover prescriptions or medicines. Skilled nursing care is covered for limited periods after a period of hospitalization, but long-term nursing care is not covered.

There are strict requirements about the time periods during which a worker may enroll in Medicare. The initial enrollment period is the period of time surrounding the beneficiary's 65th birthday. Thereafter, a beneficiary may enroll, at extra cost, during a general enrollment period, which is the first calendar quarter of a given year. In almost all cases, there is no charge to the beneficiary for the hospital insurance (Part A). There is a monthly fee for the medical insurance (Part B). A beneficiary who is enrolled in both Part A and Part B may, in most states, enroll in Part C (Medicare Advantage) plans. These are private companies, mostly Health Maintenance Organizations (HMOs) and Preferred Provider Organizations (PPOs). These managed care plans may help lower your costs of receiving medical services, or you may *get extra benefits for an additional monthly fee. You must follow the rules and procedures of these plans which may include pre-approval of certain services, and limitations on the doctors you may choose. You may also obtain prescription drug benefits under many of these plans.*

Prescription drug coverage is available under Medicare Part D. Under this option you pay a small monthly premium, which varies by plan, a co-pay and a yearly deductible which also can vary by plan and changes from year to year. Then Medicare pays 75% of the costs between the deductible and the initial benefit limit of $2,510 (2008) in drug spending. You pay 100% of the drug costs above this limit until you reach the "catastrophic threshold" ($4,050 in 2008) in out-of-pocket spending. After you have spent the out-of-pocket amount Medicare will pay about 95% of the costs. This is referred to as "catastrophic coverage."

The following questions and answers deal with some of the specifics about applying for Medicare, the costs of it, and how eligibility is determined.

Q I am from Miami, Florida. My mother-in-law is living with us. She divorced her husband after thirty years. She is 65 years old and doesn't have any income or any health insurance. I give her a house and anything she wants, but I don't know if she can get some kind of Medicaid.

A You are a very good son-in-law to provide your mother-in-law with a house and anything she wants. You may be able to buy her Medicare coverage, if you wish, even if she never worked under Social Security. Medicare has hospital insurance (Part A) and medical insurance (Part B).

Most people are eligible for Medicare Part A without a premium, if they or a spouse has 40 or more quarters of covered employment. If your mother-in-law or her husband never worked under Social Security, then she would not be eligible for this. If her ex-husband had worked for Social Security, she would eligible as an ex-wife. If neither she nor her ex-husband has the required employment, then you may purchase Medicare Part A coverage for a monthly premium of $319 per month. The Part B premium for the medical insurance portion is $54 per month.

Medicare coverage is very good, although there are some deductibles. In addition to that, you may purchase *supplemental* Medicare insurance to cover the deductibles and the elements that Medicare does not cover.

Your mother-in-law may qualify for Medicaid if she meets the requirements under state law for that program. *Medicaid* is a health insurance program for needy individuals. It is funded half by the federal government and half by the states. The states set the eligibility requirements subject to federal limitations. However, medicaid coverage is terrible. However, because it pays for only a fraction of a doctor's regular fees and many healthcare providers refuse to accept it. If you want to look into Medicaid coverage for your mother-in-law, you would have to contact the State Department of Social Services or a local welfare agency for further information about that.

Q **I will be 65 this year and I am thoroughly confused about what I have to pay, when I start paying, and how it gets paid. Does it come out automatically or do I have to do something? My husband, who is younger than I am, has me insured and he will be working for about another ten years. Do I still**

need to buy into Medicare or can I just depend on his? Would I be better off just using Medicare so he will no longer have to pay insurance for me? Sorry there are so many questions; I told you I was confused. Thank you for taking the time to address my problem.

A The first question is whether or not you have enough earnings under Social Security on your own earnings record to qualify for a retirement insurance benefit. If you have *forty quarters* of covered employment, then you will qualify for a monthly benefit, as well as Medicare Part A and Part B.

If you do not have enough quarters on your own account, you may qualify for Medicare at age 65 if your husband would be entitled to receive a Social Security benefit.

You will be eligible for a *wife's benefit* when your husband retires. You may qualify for Medicare as his wife when you are 65, even if he has not yet applied or retired, provided he is at least age 62. Your entitlement under this provision can begin with the first month in which he turns 62, even if he cannot qualify for a retirement benefit at that time because he is not age 62 throughout the month. You may qualify provided he has the required number of quarters of coverage under Social Security when he turns 62.

If your husband is not 62, or you don't have enough quarters of coverage to qualify for a retirement benefit on your own account, you may still buy into Medicare for a monthly premium, both for the hospital insurance as well as for the medical insurance. However, because your husband has a health plan that covers you, you need not do that, because the cost is quite high for the hospital insurance premium on Medicare.

As long as you are covered under your husband's health insurance program, you can wait until he attains age 62 before signing up for Medicare. However, I would suggest you go to the Social Security office to inquire about your benefits and to get your earnings record. If you have enough quarters of coverage, you may be entitled to a benefit because you are over age 62. When you go, bring your birth certificate. If your husband is at least age 62, also take your marriage certificate and your husband's birth certificate. If you are working, also bring your last year's W-2 Form. Good luck.

Q **Can a person retiring before age 65 be able to obtain Medicare Insurance Part A and B? If so, what is the monthly cost of this insurance?**

A You cannot qualify for Medicare until you turn age 65 unless you are totally disabled and receiving Social Security disability benefits for twenty-four months. You can then get the Medicare coverage in your twenty-fifth month of disability entitlement. If your primary or secondary diagnosis is ALS (also called Lou Gehrig's Disease), you can be entitled to Medicare. If you suffer from *End-Stage Renal Disease*, you may also qualify for Medicare. All others must be at least age 65 to qualify.

Q What are the new rules for the Part B Medicare monthly premium?

A The standard Part B monthly premium is $93.50 in 2007, but beginning in 2007, there is a change in the way the Part B premium is calculated. Instead of a flat rate for all, higher income people pay more, on a progressive scale. This starts with individuals with income over $80,000 (married couples with income over $160,000) and rises up to the highest amount for those with income over $200,000 ($400,000 for married couples). The increased amounts range from $105.80 to $161.40.

Q I heard that the government will give a subsidy for low income people to reduce their payments required under Part D for prescription drugs. How does this work?

A The Social Security Administration handles the applications for Part D low income subsidies. Low income means less than 150% of the Federal Poverty Level. For 2007, this comes to $15,315 for a single person household, and $20,535 for a two person family, and you can add $5,220 to the limit for each additional person in the family. The amounts are somewhat higher in Alaska and Hawaii. You may qualify for the extra help if your combined savings, investments, and real estate—not counting your home—are worth less than $11,710, if you are single, or $23,410 if you are living with your spouse. These amounts change each year. The rules are complex and cannot be discussed fully here. You should call Social Security to apply for a subsidy so that you may not have to pay a premium or deductible. Call Social Security at 1-800-772-1213 (TTY 1-800-325-0778) or visit the website at **www.socialsecurity.gov** to apply online.

Chapter 5 — SPOUSES' BENEFITS

The Social Security Act provides that wives and husbands of retired and disabled workers may collect benefits if they are age 62 or have young children of the worker in care. There is no provision for disability benefits to a wife or husband. Widows or widowers are entitled to disability benefits beginning at age 50 on their deceased spouse's account, unlike the provision for spouses of a living wage earner.

Divorced wives who are of age may also collect on the ex-husbands' accounts provided they have been divorced at least two years. In fact, the wage earner spouse may be still working, and the ex-wife may nevertheless collect on the ex's account. The payment of benefits to an ex-wife has no effect on the family maximum provisions, which place a limit on the total amount of benefits that can be paid to any one family.

Spouses' benefits are payable to the spouses of retired, as well as disabled, workers.

Q I would like to know if I will be allowed to draw off my ex-husband's Social Security. We were married thirteen years and have three children. I remarried once, for a short time, approximately a year. Does that make me ineligible to draw off my first husband's claim when I turn 63? I live in Ohio and my second husband had no income. He has been on Social Security disability for many years. Thank you.

A You will be able to receive a divorced wife's benefit on your first husband's account providing you are not married at the time you make the application. Additionally, you can collect the ex-wife's benefit beginning at age 62. You do not have to wait until age 63. What makes an ex-wife's benefit even better than a regular wife's benefit is that the husband need not be retired. As long as he is eligible, even if he has not yet retired or applied for Social Security, you can collect an ex-wife's benefit on his account. You cannot collect on your second husband's account because you were not married for at least ten years.

Q My sister, a widow, was just awarded disability benefits on her deceased husband's account retroactive to age 58. She is not yet 60. She is receiving 71½% of the full benefit as if she were 60 years of age. Other disabled workers receive a 100% benefit when they take early retirement due to disability. It seems unjust that she should get only 71½%.

Also, Social Security people have told her that her benefit will never increase to 100%, even at age 65. This seems even more unfair and, in fact, the agency's own manual suggests that the benefit does increase to 100% at age 65. Is it correct that her benefit is calculated at only 71½% now and does it increase to 100% at age 65?

A A disabled widow is entitled to receive widow's benefits earlier than the normal age 60, provided she is totally disabled and at least age 50. In that event, the amount of the disabled widow's benefit is the same as if she were age 60. At age 60, a widow is entitled to 71½% of the worker's full benefit. Your sister is receiving the correct percentage at this time.

You state that other disabled workers receive a 100% benefit when they take early retirement due to disability. That is true when they receive benefits on their *own* wage record. It may be unjust that a disabled widow receives only 71½%, but that is the way the law was designed. The answer to that is to have the law changed if Congress has the will to do so. However, it is unlikely that will change because there are serious concerns about the long-term viability of the Social Security program and any increase in benefits at this time is unlikely.

It is true that the widow's benefit will never increase beyond the 71½%, even when your sister turns 65, because she has been receiving it all along. This applies to all beneficiaries.

You say that the Social Security manual suggests that the benefit does increase to 100% at full retirement age. I think what you are thinking about there is the possibility that she could convert to a benefit on her own work record at full retirement age without the age reduction. If she had worked and earned money on her own account, she could do that if the benefit would be higher, but that only applies when there are two different benefits involved, not just the one. It appears that the benefit calculation is correct and the widow's benefit will not increase at full retirement age.

Q **I was married for twenty-six years and have been told a variety of answers to this question. Can I collect part of my ex-spouse's Social Security? If yes, at what age for me? I am 61, he is 74. What happens if I remarry? My ex-spouse is totally disabled, does this affect the answer?**

A You can receive an ex-wife's benefit beginning at age 62. Your benefits as an ex-wife will terminate if you remarry, unless you marry your ex-husband or unless you get married to an individual who is entitled to certain kinds of Social Security benefits including:

- widower's benefit;
- father's benefit;
- disabled adult child benefit;
- divorced spouse benefit; or,
- parents benefits.

✐**NOTE:** If you remarry an individual entitled to regular Social Security retirement or disability, your benefits will also terminate. It makes no difference that your ex-spouse now is totally disabled.

Q I live in the state of Texas. A friend of mine says she draws half of her husband's Social Security and he still gets his full amount of his benefits. My question is why can't I receive half of my husband's since his is much greater than mine?

A You should be able to receive benefits on your husband's account if you are at least age 62 and if you have been married for at least one year to the worker. If you are entitled to benefits on your own account, you may be eligible to receive the difference up to one half of your husband's full unreduced benefit amount. If you are not receiving these benefits and you are over 62, I would suggest that you contact the Social Security office immediately to claim these benefits.

Q I was married for thirty-three years. If I remarry, will I still be able to draw my first husband's Social Security?

A You do not say how the marriage ended, or if your first husband is alive. If you were divorced, you may receive benefits on his account because you were married for more than ten years. If he is alive, your benefits will terminate upon remarriage. If he is deceased, remarriage after age 60 will not affect benefits on his account.

Q I was married just short of eleven years to my former husband. I remarried four years later, but divorced number two within two years. I have been unmarried now for more than twenty years. Husband number one remarried shortly after our divorce, and both he and his wife are now retired. He and I are the same age. When I start to collect Social Security at age 65, must I collect on my earnings only, or can I collect against husband number one? I was married to him more than the ten-year requirement, and he made a lot more money than I ever did. Or am I not eligible to collect against his Social Security because of his new wife, or because I once remarried for a short period of time?

A You may collect benefits on your ex-husband's account even though he remarried and you remarried, because your second marriage has ended. To be eligible as an ex-wife, you need only be unmarried when you apply. Of course, you must meet the other requirements that apply to wife benefits, such as him being eligible and your benefit on your own account being less than one-half of his. As you noted, your marriage to the worker had to last at least ten years, which yours did. By the way, you don't have to wait till age 65 to collect. You may collect at age 62, if your earnings permit, providing that he is also at least 62.

Q When can an ex-wife draw Social Security from her ex-spouse? Do you have to have been married for a certain amount of years? Is there a time line from the time of divorce until the time you can draw? If your ex-spouse was married with children previously, is that the only one who can draw on Social Security benefits?

A A divorced wife who was married to the ex for at least ten years *consecutively* before the divorce became final (you cannot add up years from a previous marriage to the same man, unless you remarried in the same calendar year of the divorce, or the year immediately following the year of the divorce) can collect a divorced wife's benefit at age 62, if she is unmarried and her benefit on her own work record is not higher.

☞**NOTE:** Even if the ex-husband has not retired, the wife can collect on his account if he otherwise would be eligible (i.e., age 62 with enough work credits).

You must be divorced at least two years before the application to collect when the ex is still working. The two-year requirement does not apply if the ex-husband is retired.

Q I had been married for twenty years before my husband and I got a divorce. Two years ago, I remarried. When I reach 62 years of age, in two more years, am I eligible to claim Social Security benefits from my former husband? Thank you.

A No, only as a wife under your new husband's account.

Q I have a question for you. I live in the state of Idaho, and have lived with my boyfriend for seventeen years. We are not legally married. Although Idaho did have a common-law marriage for years, it was recently ruled out just a few years ago. My boyfriend (who has never been legally married) and I have bought our home and property together, it's all in both of our names. My question is, am I eligible, should anything happen to him, to receive benefits? Thank you so much.

A If the law of the state where you live does not recognize your relationship as a legal marriage, neither does Social Security. You are not eligible for any benefits on his account unless you "tie the knot." If you are not eligible for benefits on your own work record, you stand to lose a lot of money in Social Security benefits that you may otherwise collect as a legal wife or widow.

In your case, you may have a valid common-law marriage because Idaho recognized such marriages if contracted before January 1, 1996. To be a valid marriage, you must both have been free to marry when the marriage began, and intended to be married, as opposed to just living together. It is difficult to prove a common-law marriage after one of the spouses dies. If you are concerned about this (as you should be), why don't you marry in a legal ceremony?

Q My father passed away in 1983. At the time, there was a sibling that received benefits because she was young. My mother is now 57 years old. When does she begin collecting survivor benefits?

A Your mother may collect as an "aged widow" at age 60, or sooner, if she is totally disabled.

Q I am a housewife and have been for twenty-two of my twenty-four years of marriage. I have begun to worry about my Social Security benefits because I haven't paid in very many quarters. I would estimate that I have only paid in three or four years' worth of quarters. What happens to me at Social Security retirement time? Will I qualify for benefits both under Social Security and Medicare? I have heard that my husband covers me in this with his work history, but I want to be sure. Thank you for your attention to this very important concern of mine.

A Don't worry, because you are entitled to wife's benefits on your husband's account. Because you are married more than ten years, these benefits are *vested*—you get them even if you become divorced. You are entitled to one-half of your husband's primary insurance amount, the amount he would receive at full retirement age. If you are under *Full Retirement Age* when you become eligible, the benefit is reduced for each month before full retirement age. For those born in 1938 (1940 for widows), two extra months are added— *Full Retirement Age* (FRA) is age 65 and two months. The FRA increases each year after that, according to a schedule. (It is age 66 for people born between January 2, 1943, and January 1, 1955.)

You are eligible for wife's benefits at age 62, but only if your husband is receiving benefits. If he should die, you are eligible for widow's benefits beginning with age 60, but again, these benefits are reduced if you are under *Full Retirement Age*. Unlike the wife's benefit, the unreduced widow's benefit is equal to your husband's full benefit. You may be eligible for a disabled widow's benefit beginning at age 50, if you should become totally disabled.

Q I am entitled to my ex-husband's Social Security. Somebody told me they take the last five years of his income. What if he doesn't show any work history for the last five years but he has worked the last forty years? Can I still collect part of his?

A Yes, if you are otherwise eligible. Social Security drops the lowest five years in calculating the benefit amount. As long as the worker has at least forty quarters of coverage (this can be spread out; it doesn't have to be consecutive), he or she is eligible for benefits. This includes ex-wives and ex-husbands if they meet the other requirements, such as being married at least ten years before the divorce and unmarried now. Once eligibility is established, then the amount of the benefit is computed, and that's where the five years of low earnings are dropped.

✏**NOTE:** There are different rules for disability benefits.

Q How do I handle this? I have a *common-law* husband and he is 58 now. I am only 46. I was wondering what we need to do as we approach retirement age. Do I have to file any forms, change my name, etc.? Thanks.

A Going through with a ceremonial marriage would be best. "Common-law husband" means, in most states, no husband. The laws of all but a dozen states have long ago abolished common-law marriage. Social Security does recognize a common-law marriage only if the state in which it was contracted recognizes such a marriage.

To be valid in those few states that recognize it, there must be a true intent to be married, not just an intent to live together until further notice, and the parties must be free to marry. Prior marriage, if not lawfully terminated, will bar a common-law marriage. It can be very difficult to prove common-law marriage, especially if one party is deceased.

Simply *living with* entitles you to nothing but major headaches. Social Security does not recognize a simple "living together" relationship as valid for wife's or widow's benefits. Perhaps you should make your marriage official with the proper documents.

Q **If my husband should die, would I be entitled to the full amount of Social Security benefits he received while alive, or would I only be able to get my personal benefit, which I now get on my own earnings? The amount my husband receives is $300 more than I receive. Thank you.**

A You will get the amount your husband receives, subject to possible age reduction if you are under full retirement age.

Q I was 62 on December 7, 2001. My past work history shows that I have earned more than forty quarters. I am drawing a retirement from federal civil service and the U.S. Army. I have not applied for Social Security as I have been told I would only receive around 50% because of my two other federal retirements. Is this true?

My ex-wife (we were married fourteen years) works at General Motors and has over forty quarters. Neither of us are married. When she reaches 62, can I draw on her Social Security and not be reduced by 50% because of my other federal retirements? When a person draws on an ex-spouse's Social Security, does that reduce the ex-spouse's Social Security benefits? Thank you for your time.

A Okay, that's at least three questions. But as a veteran, you're entitled in my book.

Let's start with your federal and military pensions. These have no effect on your Social Security retirement benefits. The only reduction will be for age (if you take it at age 62), at approximately 20% off the full benefit. If your ex-wife has a primary insurance amount (the unreduced benefit) high enough that one-half of it is greater than your primary insurance amount, then you can be entitled to the difference between yours and one-half of hers. But that difference will be reduced for age if you are under *Full Retirement Age* when she turns 62.

The bad news is that two-thirds of your government pension will be deducted from the spouse's benefit. If there is anything left (unlikely), it will then be added to your benefit on your own account. You can collect this even if she is still working, and even if she has remarried. Your entitlement on her account will not affect her benefits.

Q I have been married to Robert for over thirty years. I am disabled and separated, but not legally. I need some help from him and he won't help me. What do I do? I know he is getting his Social Security. I married him in 1967 in Waukegan, Illinois, at the Lake County Courthouse. I was 20; he was 21. Please help me.

A You do not appear eligible for any Social Security benefits at present. There are no disabled wife's benefits provided. At age 62, you will be eligible for a wife's benefit, which will be 50% of his primary insurance amount, reduced for age if you take it under *Full Retirement Age*. Because you were born in 1947, *Full Retirement Age* will be age 66, so the wife's benefit will be reduced 30% at age 62 for you.

If your husband should die, you would be eligible for a widow's benefit at age 60. If you are totally disabled, you would be eligible for a disabled widow's benefit if you are at least age 50, which you are.

The amount of the disabled widow's benefits payable for age 60 is equal to the reduced widow's benefit amount at age 60, which is 71½% of the primary insurance amount. I would also suggest that you contact an attorney to find out if you have legal rights as a wife to support and maintenance from your husband. Best of wishes to you.

Q We are citizens of the United States but our home is in Mexico. My question is—are Social Security payments *community property* in the event of a divorce?

A No, at least as determined by the Social Security Administration. Social security benefits are payable to each individual, provided that the eligibility requirements are met. In the case of a divorce, a divorced spouse is entitled to receive benefits as a divorced wife or husband, provided that she or he was married for at least ten years immediately before the divorce became final. Additionally, the divorced spouse must not be remarried, must file an application, and meet the age requirement of age 62.

Warning

In fact, a divorced spouse has an advantage over a married spouse because the divorcee can receive benefits as long as the worker is over 62, even if the worker has not yet retired or even filed for Social Security. However, to take advantage of this provision, the spouse must be divorced for at least two continuous years before qualifying for these independent benefits.

Remarriage of a divorced spouse will terminate entitlement to benefits unless the marriage is to an individual entitled to survivor benefits, disabled adult child benefits, parents' benefits, or divorced spouse's benefits. Marriage to a regular Social Security retirement beneficiary does not qualify.

Q If I wait until I'm 65 and some months old to retire, will the amount I draw on my ex-husband's account be diminished because he retired at 62? We were married for thirty-one years.

A Your benefit as an ex-wife will not be reduced for age if you take it at *Full Retirement Age*, even if your husband took a reduced retirement benefit. The way the benefit is figured is to start with the husband's primary insurance amount and divide that in half. That 50% benefit is payable at *Full Retirement Age* to you. It is only reduced if you are under *Full Retirement Age* when you become entitled to it.

✏**NOTE:** If you are entitled to a retirement benefit on your own account and your primary insurance amount is greater than 50% of your husband's primary amount, you will not be entitled to any spouse or ex-spouse benefit.

Q My wife is ten years younger than I. She has worked and paid into her own Social Security account for about eleven years, but has since become a housewife and will probably remain that way. When I begin to draw Social Security benefits for retirement, does my wife begin to draw at the same time or does she wait until she is 62?

A She will have to wait until she is 62. At that time, she may be eligible for benefits on her own earnings record. Because, as you say, she has worked for about eleven years, she will have the required number of quarters of coverage (forty). The amount of her benefit will be calculated based on a reduction if she takes it at age 62. If her own primary insurance amount is less than one half of your primary amount, she will be eligible to receive a portion of the difference between her full amount and one half of your full amount. The difference will be reduced as well because she will be under *Full Retirement Age* at that time. She would be eligible to receive a widow's benefit at age 60, if you should die. She could also receive it after age 50, if she were totally disabled.

Q I was told that since I was married for fifteen years and had two children with my ex-husband, that I am entitled to collect Social Security under him at a certain age. I am 55; he is 56. I am and have been on disability and out of work for over five years now. Most of my married life I stayed home and brought up our children. So what I collect now on Social Security disability and workers' compensation is not much at all. What do I have to do and when do I get this set up to see what my options are in the future? Thank you.

A You would be eligible for a divorced wife's benefit when you turn 62, even if your husband does not retire. The amount of that benefit is one half of his primary insurance amount less, your primary amount as a Social Security disability beneficiary. The difference will be further reduced if you take it at age 62, because of the age reduction. If your ex-husband should die, you presently would be eligible for a disabled widow's benefit if that would be higher than your current Social Security disability benefit. A disabled widow's benefit is 71½% of the deceased workers' primary insurance amount.

Because your ex-husband is still alive, you need to do nothing at present. If you should learn that he dies, then you should apply immediately for the disabled widow's benefit or if you are then aged 60, for the regular widow's benefit. You are entitled because you were married for more than ten years.

If he does not die before you turn 62, then you should file for benefits as an independently entitled divorced wife. You should go to the Social Security office about three months before your 62nd birthday with your marriage certificate and divorce decree as well as your birth certificate. Best wishes to you.

Q **At our last coffee break, we were discussing divorced spouses drawing Social Security benefits from their ex-spouses. What are the qualifications for this? Does the ex-spouse have to be retired and drawing off Social Security in order for the other ex-spouse to draw Social Security? What happens to the new spouse's retirement from the Social Security if the ex-spouse draws from the ex-spouse's Social Security number?**

A Divorced spouses may be independently entitled to Social Security benefits as a divorced wife or divorced husband on the ex-spouse's account. The spouses must have been married at least ten years and must be divorced at least two years before the application is filed. Beginning at age 62, the ex-spouse can collect and will receive the same benefit amount as a married spouse. The amount the ex-spouse gets will have no effect on the worker's benefits or any other dependents (such as a wife or children) receiving on his account.

To claim these benefits you will need your marriage certificate, your divorce decree, as well as your birth certificate.

✏️**NOTE:** If you have earnings on your own account, you may be entitled to those benefits. If they are higher than the benefits as an ex-spouse, you will only receive the higher retirement benefit on your account.

If your own benefit is less than the ex-spouse's benefit, then you will receive the difference between the benefit on your account and as an ex-spouse. It will all be paid in one check.

Q **I want to know if I am entitled to my husband's Social Security if we get divorced and he marries someone else after he starts getting Social Security. From what I understand, he has applied for Social Security and is waiting for his check. We have been married for thirty-nine years, but he has lived with someone else and plans to marry her soon. Am I entitled to this? And what happens after he dies, if he dies before me? I would appreciate any information you can give me.**

A Because you were married at least ten years, you will be entitled to widow's benefits in the event of your husband's death, if you are at least age 60 years old or 50 if you are totally disabled.

You did not say when you were divorced. In order to be entitled as an ex-spouse to the wife's benefits, you must be divorced at least two years. If you are divorced at least two years, then you will be able to collect as an ex-spouse the same as if you were still married.

Q I will be 59 this year and so will my wife. The question is: When I reach retirement age, will my wife be eligible for any benefits due to my retirement? I realize this covers a broad field. Will she be eligible for any percentages of the benefits even though she does not have 40 quarters of earnings? She basically has been a housewife. If I pass away, will she be eligible for any benefits, and if so, what benefits and in what amounts? Will she be eligible for Medicare or Medicaid when she reaches age 65? Thank you for any help you can give.

A Your wife will be entitled to receive a benefit on your account both as a wife, and in the event of your death, as a widow. The amount of her benefit as a wife is 50% of your primary insurance amount. If she becomes entitled to it before *Full Retirement Age*, it will be reduced for age according to how old she is at the time when she first begins receiving it.

If you die before her, she will be entitled to receive a widow's benefit on your account. The amount of that benefit will be the same monthly benefit you receive during your life. She will be entitled to Medicare at age 65.

Q Could you give some information concerning spouses' Social Security benefits? I will explain to you my situation. I have been living with a man for thirty-four years. We never married. He was married in the past and never legally divorced from his first wife. She had abandoned him at the time I met him. So all these years I am with this man and he never divorced her. So I would like to know, being that she did abandon him but is to this day legally married to him, is she entitled to all of his Social Security benefits?

This man that I have lived with has decided to divorce this person even though she has never been found. Now when he does divorce her and decides to marry me, how will his Social Security benefits work when he passes on? Is she entitled to the whole amount of benefits or will I receive a partial amount of it? How does that work? I also heard rumors about being married ten years to a spouse to receive their Social Security benefits at the time they pass on. Is that true? Could you please let me know some information about this?

A The legal wife of your "friend" is entitled to Social Security benefits as his wife, and if he dies, as a widow. In order for her to collect as a wife, he must be entitled to Social Security benefits and she must be at least age 62 or have a child of his in her care. If he divorces her, then the ex-wife can be independently entitled on his account, even if he does not retire and provided they have been divorced at least two years.

Because they were married for more than ten years, she would also qualify as a surviving divorced wife in the event he divorced her. If he does not divorce her, she will be entitled as a widow on his account.

If you are not married to him, you will be entitled to *nothing* on his account. If he should divorce her and marry you, you would be entitled to a widow's benefit in the event of his death if you are married at least nine months before he dies, unless the death was accidental. There are some other exceptions, but nine months is the general *duration of marriage* rule. If he marries you, you must be married at least one year before you can file for benefits as his wife, although there are some exceptions to this as well, such as having a child together.

Q **If I am older than my husband and start drawing on my own earnings, can I draw on his account when he reaches retirement age if that is more than what I can get on my own?**

A Yes. Your benefit will be calculated based on your age at the time you become entitled to a benefit on his account. It doesn't matter if you are older than he is. If a benefit as his wife is higher than the benefit on your own account, you can collect the difference. This would be added to your payment amount and you will receive one check for both your own benefit and the extra amount on his account.

Q **My wife was divorced from her ex-husband over ten years ago, but she never changed her last name due to carelessness on her part. Last Friday, I took her to the Social Security Administration office to apply for a change of name and we were told that she must have an ID with her previous last name on it.**

This is kind of difficult given the length of time and the circumstances surrounding the divorce. We presented various IDs showing that her name was changed by the given authorities:

- driver's license from the state of Florida showing her maiden name issued after the divorce;
- voting registration card issued after the divorce;
- U.S. passport issued by the federal government after the divorce; and,
- current marriage certificate issued by the state of Florida showing her maiden name and current last name.

They still have insisted that she must have an ID card showing her previous married name. There has to be a better way to do this. She doesn't have an ID showing her previous last name and given the circumstances surrounding her divorce, I am not about to ask her ex-husband, provided that he is even still alive.

A Try to get a copy of the divorce decree that will identify her with her married name and her maiden name. Usually the divorce decree will specifically authorize the use of the maiden name and the decree would identify your wife with her then married name. If you continue to run into problems at the Social Security office, even with the decree, I would suggest that you speak to a supervisor at the office. If that is unavailing, then I would suggest that you speak with your congressperson and seek help through your elected official. This often is very effective.

Q I am 63 and plan to retire in either January or February. My retirement benefit from state employment should not be over $1,800 per month. My deceased ex-husband remarried, but I understand that I am still entitled to his benefits. Is this correct and, if so, can I get an idea as to what it would be?

I also need to know if I have money invested, but keep it in the investment and use only the interest to add to my retirement, will that hinder the money I am entitled to get from my ex-husband? Because of the offset, I hear several different opinions and since it is getting close, I would like to make some plans or at least be able to know what I am up against. Thanks.

A You will be entitled to receive a benefit on your deceased ex-husband if you were married for at least ten years before the divorce. The amount of that benefit will depend on his primary insurance amount. You will be able to receive 100% of that primary insurance amount if you are of *Full Retirement Age.*

The offset you are talking about is the government pension offset. This provision requires a deduction from any Social Security benefits you may receive as a wife or a widow. The amount of the deduction is two-thirds of your state pension. The deduction applies only if your state employment is not covered by Social Security.

For Example:

If your state pension is $1,800, then the deduction would be $1,200 from your Social Security benefits. The amount of your Social Security benefit, if you receive it at Full Retirement Age, and if your ex-husband had very high earnings, could exceed that offset amount. For instance, a maximum benefit for a worker in the year 2007 is approximately $1,960 per month. If that were the amount of your husband's primary insurance benefit, you would be able to receive the difference between that and $1,200.

Q I was married to a man back in the 1960s and we separated six years later. We were never divorced. I found out that he died a couple of years ago and would like to know if I am entitled to Social Security benefits. Thank you.

A As the legal wife of the worker, you are entitled to benefits on his account if you meet the other requirements. For a widow this generally means that you are at least age 60 and not married. You may remarry after age 60—this will be disregarded. If you are totally disabled, you may receive *disabled widow's benefits* beginning with age 50.

Q My future husband is 62 next month. He will be receiving Social Security benefits soon. He was married to his first wife for fifteen years. They both worked during that time, but he made more money. They have two adult children ages 35 and 36. His wife has never remarried and will be 62 in the year 2005. In the following years, my future husband married wife number two for three years and wife number three for three months.

My question is: I am 42 years of age—what, if any, benefits would I be entitled to when we marry? In addition, would his first wife be entitled to any benefits? Would our marriage compromise her possible benefits, if any? In short, I am fond of wife number one. What kind of benefits are we both entitled to? Would our marriage compromise her future benefits? Thanks in advance.

A You will be eligible for a wife's benefit on your husband's account when you turn 62, if he should still be alive at that time. If not, you would be eligible for a widow's benefit, which could begin at age 60, or even at age 50 if you should be totally disabled. His first wife will be entitled to ex-wife's benefits on his account when she turns 62 because she was married to him for at least ten years. Because of this ten-year duration of marriage requirement, wives number two and three will not be entitled to receive benefits as ex-wives on his account. The first wife will not lose any benefits by reason of your marriage.

Q I got married not long ago and I wonder if there was something I had to change with the Social Security department before I could do my taxes. Is there or am I fine to go ahead with our taxes?

A You can change your name for Social Security purposes. You may contact the Social Security Administration to obtain a new card. You will need to show them your marriage certificate to show the new name. A new card will be issued. You should not wait for this to file your taxes because I don't believe the IRS would be very understanding. Eventually, the records will be corrected.

Q I was recently married and need to know how to change my name with Social Security. Please advise.

A You must go to the Social Security office with evidence of your maiden name and your marriage certificate, which will show your new name. Make sure you bring the original documents or copies certified by the agency issuing the certificate. You cannot make your own photocopies. Social Security will give you your original documents back.

Q My husband is a British citizen who has been living and working in the United States for fourteen years. He obtained his alien card when we moved here in 1988 and has had Social Security deducted from his paychecks. Will he be eligible to receive Social Security benefits without becoming a U.S. citizen?

A Yes, provided he has sufficient quarters of coverage under the Social Security system, which it appears that he does. Additionally, his Social Security credits that he may have earned in Great Britain will also be available for use in the calculation of his benefit.

Chapter 6

CHILDREN

Social Security law provides that the young children of retired, disabled, or deceased workers may collect a child's benefit up until age 18. At one time, benefits were continued to age 22 if the child was a full-time college student. That provision was eliminated some time ago, although if the child is still in high school, he or she may collect benefits until attaining age 19. Children disabled before age 22 may collect as disabled adult children.

Children of various kinds can be eligible in addition to the natural children. Adopted children, stepchildren, and even equitably adopted children can receive benefits. In certain circumstances, grandchildren can collect benefits on the grandparent's account, provided that the parents are deceased or disabled prior to the grandparent's entitlement.

Because a child, generally speaking, cannot take care of his or her own interests, Social Security ordinarily will pay the benefits to a representative payee on behalf of the child. Usually this is the natural parent living with the child, although that is not always the case.

This chapter will discuss the various circumstances and issues pertaining to benefits payable to children.

Q I am 16 years old and my father is 67 years old and retired. My father receives extra money from Social Security because I am still his dependent, and we were informed that if I were to start working and earn a paycheck, that his extra money from Social Security would be cut off. Because of this information, I cannot work and earn a measly teenager's paycheck. Recently, I was informed that a law had passed that stated that retired people from ages 65 to 69 could earn as much income as they wanted without it interfering with Social Security benefits. Is this true, and if so, does this mean that I can now work without my father's extra benefits being cut off?

A It's true that your earnings affect the child's benefit your father receives on your behalf as a minor child, but your earnings will not affect his own benefit. If your earnings exceed $12,960 per year for 2007, then you would lose $1 for each $2 over the limit. Under the new change in the law, your father's earnings will have no effect on his benefits because he is over full retirement age, but you are still subject to the earnings test.

☞**NOTE:** If you are making a "measly teenager's" pay of under $12,960 for the year, it will have no effect on the child's benefit.

Q My daughter is 18 years old and starting college. Her father is receiving Social Security. Can she draw Social Security benefits while she is going to college until she is 21?

A   Benefits for college students were eliminated many years ago. Children's benefits are payable only for those under age 18. Benefits will continue only while the child is in high school (not college), and only up to age 19. Accredited home school programs may also qualify.

Q   I just had a baby. This is my first child and I don't know how to obtain a Social Security number or a card for my child. I would appreciate it if you could let me know what I have to do. Thank you.

A   Congratulations! If you want to obtain a Social Security number for your new darling, you must contact the Social Security Administration. They have a toll-free number, 800-772-1213. You will need the birth certificate. You must complete a form, an SS-5. You can download this from **www.ssa.gov/online/ss-5.html**. You will have to make a personal visit to the Social Security office. You can find the nearest office by calling the toll-free number or online at **www.ssa.gov/locator.** You must take an *original, certified* copy of the birth certificate with you.

Q   My son was receiving survivor benefits after his father passed away. His benefits stopped when he turned 19, even though he was in learning disability in high school and did not graduate until the June before he turned 20 in August. Should he have received the benefits until he graduated high school?

A The benefits continue only to the end of the semester in which the child turns 19. But if the child is totally disabled from doing any *substantial gainful work,* benefits may continue for as long as the disability lasts.

Q My husband's nephew has unfortunately lost both his parents within the last few years and is collecting Social Security. His fraternal grandmother has custody of him as of now. Our nephew has approached us and wants to live with us. That is no problem, but my question is, if we legally adopt him so that he could be covered under my health insurance, dental, and optical, would he still receive the Social Security benefits to be put away for college and emergencies, or do we have to keep just custody of him so he doesn't lose his Social Security benefits? He is currently 13 years old. Thank you for your consideration to this matter.

A Adoption does not terminate a child's benefits once they are established. Your nephew will continue to be entitled to his Social Security benefits even after the adoption. Best wishes for you and your nephew.

Q My daughter is 15 and her natural father passed away. She was adopted by my current husband. My husband was able to adopt her on the grounds of abandonment. Her natural father never paid his child support. Is she eligible for Social Security benefits?

A Your daughter cannot collect on the deceased natural father's account because she was adopted by your husband before the father's death, and therefore is not considered to be the father's dependent. If the natural father were living with the child or supporting the child, she could collect on his account, but that is not the case here. Another exception is if the deceased had been entitled to disability under Social Security up until his death or entitlement to retirement benefits. Otherwise, your daughter cannot collect on the natural father's account.

Q **My mother just recently passed away, and she was receiving Social Security benefits. I have been told by several people that since my mother passed away, and I am a full-time college student, I can receive supplemental security. Is this true?**

A I am sorry to hear about the loss of your mom. Unfortunately, you may not collect Social Security benefits any longer as a college student. The law only allows continuation of benefits for secondary school (not college) students till age 19, while still in high school.

You asked about *supplemental* benefits. I think you are confusing terms here, which many people do. Supplemental Security Income (SSI) is a federal welfare program for the disabled (of any age, including children), elderly (65+), and the blind. These benefits are administered by the Social Security Administration, but the benefits come from general federal tax revenues, not the Social Security payroll taxes or funds. Additionally, many states supplement the SSI payments.

Social Security benefits are paid based on a wage earner's *contributions* (government-speak for payroll taxes) and are paid at retirement or disability to the wage earner and dependents, and at death to a surviving spouse and minor children. At one time these benefits could continue until age 22 for full-time college students, but the law changed several years ago.

Q I need information on entitlement and termination rules for stepchildren who draw Social Security disability. I need to know if laws have changed to say that stepchildren no longer are entitled if mother and stepfather are divorced. I pulled up 1995 laws, and there is supposed to be an amendment after 1995 that states that they are no longer entitled, but I cannot find this. It's very important. I need this as soon as possible. Thank you for your time.

A Current regulations do not provide for termination upon divorce—so benefits should continue.

Q My grandson's mother died. His father, my son, became the official parent. However, the stepfather set up and received the child's Social Security benefits. How was this possible without some form of proof citing him as the legal custodian? And how do I go about rectifying this injustice? The child chose to stay with his stepfather, but he spends just as much time with me. I should say here, the boy is 15 years old.

A Your son, as the natural father, would have preference over the stepfather for purposes of being the payee for a minor child, provided he "demonstrates strong concern for the child's well being." He must go to the Social Security office with proof of the relationship. If he contributes support, proof of that as well. He must apply to be the representative payee.

Q **Can grandparents whose grandchild is in the home and has been for several months be eligible for Social Security benefits when the grandparents draw benefits? This child has not been adopted by the grandparents and the grandparents have temporary custody of the child.**

A A grandchild can qualify as a "child" on the grandparent's account if the child's natural or adoptive parents are either deceased or disabled when the grandparent became entitled to Social Security. The child cannot qualify if the parents were alive or not disabled at the time of the grandparent's entitlement. A great-grandchild cannot qualify under this provision.

Q **I live in Illinois. My daughter's boyfriend died back in November. They have a 16-month-old daughter. He also has two other children from a previous marriage, but my daughter's child is the youngest. My daughter did fill out all the necessary paperwork, and presented all the documents that were needed to claim Social Security benefits for their daughter. Everything is in order.**

Till this day, she has not received anything; however, the other two children are receiving benefits and my daughter and his ex-wife went to the Social Security office on the same day. When my daughter calls to inquire, they can't tell her too much of anything except that she will be getting it. She asks for the number to the payment center and they said they couldn't give her that information. How can she find out more information about what's going on with this money?

A Because your daughter's child is the illegitimate child of the deceased worker, Social Security requires proof of the relationship before awarding benefits. The other children were born in wedlock and, therefore, automatically are presumed to be the worker's children. The additional documentation requirements are probably the reason for the delay. The official determination of *paternity* requires extra time and paperwork to verify the paternity of the child.

Q I recently did blood testing and found out that my father is who I thought. Well, my Dad died a year after I was born. I moved in with my sister who is my legal guardian. I have been awarded $15,000 of Social Security benefits for back money and will receive $900 a month until I am 18. I need a car and to move out and I would like to have some of my own money for necessities and save the rest for college. My sister flat out told me she has control of the money. I am writing wondering if there is any way legally she cannot spend my money and I can get all of it from her when I turn 18. I personally don't think it's fair.

A Social Security will not pay benefits directly to a minor where a legal guardian has been appointed. Because you are under 18 and have a legal guardian appointed, Social Security must pay your benefits to your legal guardian, in this case your sister. She is under the legal duty to conserve your funds that she receives for you and to use them only for your current needs including food, clothing, and shelter. Any extra money or the past due money that she has received for you must be maintained in a special account. That means you must be named as the beneficiary.

The Social Security regulations require her to keep the money invested with *minimum* risk and all investments must be held in trust for you. The funds should be deposited in an *interest bearing* account or *dividend bearing* account in a bank, trust company, or credit union insured under federal or state law. The interest belongs to you and not to your sister.

Furthermore, your sister, as your representative payee, must make periodic accounting to the Social Security Administration to make sure that she is not misusing your funds. When you turn 18, you will be entitled to the accumulated money and then if you wish, you can buy a car of your own choosing.

Q I was wondering how to claim fraud on my father. I am no longer living with him and he is accepting Social Security for me even though I am not there. Also, is it possible for me to receive the money seeing as how I am independent? Thank you for your time.

A Generally, a child under age 18 is presumed incapable of receiving Social Security benefits and a payee is appointed. There are some exceptions to this, however. If you are considered emancipated under state law, you are presumed to be capable of receiving your own benefits. If there is a court-appointed legal guardian for you, then the guardian should be receiving the benefits. If there is no legal guardian and you are living alone and are self-supporting, then you may also receive the benefits yourself. I would suggest that you go to your local Social Security office to discuss this further. If your father has misused funds received on your behalf, you will have to make an *accounting* to Social Security.

Q **I am a 16-year-old female having many family problems at home. I am going to move out with someone of the age of 20. How would my benefits work when this happens? I am going to school to get my G.E.D. and I am going to start a job to pay for some of the things I need. Social Security is to pay for food, shelter, clothing, and medical bills. I would still need this when I move out to help pay for such things. Would it be possible for the person with whom I am living to get the check?**

A I would recommend that you seriously reconsider your decision to move out of your family home especially if the "someone of the age of 20" is your boyfriend and you are not getting married. Although your Social Security benefits would end if you got married, I think your problems would be much greater if you enter into a "living with" arrangement especially at your young age.

The Social Security benefit payable to you as a child will continue until you turn age 18. If you are in school (other than college), the benefit may continue until you are age 19. The amount of the benefit is based solely on the earnings record of the worker on whose account you receive the benefit, which would be either a disabled, retired, or deceased parent.

The benefit is not based on your needs for food, shelter, clothing, or medical bills. If you are an *emancipated* minor, you may receive the benefits directly yourself, but Social Security would have to investigate the situation. The "someone" could apply to be your representative payee, but Social Security would have to make a determination that that would be in your best interests. I seriously doubt that such a conclusion would be reached.

Once again, I strongly recommend that you reconsider moving away from the home. Although you are having problems at home, they are likely to be far less than the problems you will face if you enter into a "living with" arrangement.

Q My husband currently receives disability benefits and his son receives money off of his benefits. We were told that stepchildren can also collect from these benefits. Can you clarify this question?

A Stepchildren of a disabled worker can receive benefits on his account. The stepchild must be dependent on the worker and the marriage of the parent to the worker must have lasted at least one year.

The benefits will stop if the parents should divorce at a later date. I would suggest that you go to your Social Security office immediately to file benefits for the stepchildren. When you go, make sure you bring their birth certificates and your marriage certificate to the worker.

Q **In December, my father died. Since then I have been receiving Social Security checks. I just turned 18 in March and had to call the Social Security office in Indiana, where I live, and tell them that I had turned 18. Then the service representative told me that the checks would stop in May when I graduated. My mom and I had always thought that the checks would continue through college until the age of 21 or until I stopped going to school. So can you please tell us why my checks will stop in May? Thanks.**

A Many years ago, Social Security was changed to eliminate college student benefits. Child's benefits no longer are payable after the child turns age 18 unless the child is in high school. In that case, the benefits may continue until the child turns 19 and if the 19th birthday is during a school year, the benefits can continue until the end of the semester. College does not count, so if you are graduating from high school this year in May, that is why the benefits will stop.

Chapter 7 — APPLYING FOR BENEFITS

Social Security law places restrictions on when a claimant may apply for benefits. The restrictions relate both to the future prospective life of the application as well as the retroactive period in the past for which the application may be effective. As a general rule, when you apply for Social Security benefits, you must produce the necessary evidence to show that you are entitled.

In the case of retirement benefits, you must prove your age by means of a birth or baptismal certificate. If such certificates are not available, secondary proof of age may be submitted and accepted by Social Security such as passports, naturalization papers, and other official documents. You should also bring your last two years' W-2 forms to establish your recent earnings because they may not be reflected on Social Security's records for some time.

If you are applying as a wife or as a husband, you should bring your marriage certificate. If you are applying for any of your children, you should bring their birth certificates.

Persons applying for disability benefits will need their birth certificates as well as the names and addresses of all their treating physicians. It is not necessary to bring the medical records with you, but you are certainly entitled to submit whatever records you wish.

Survivor benefits depend on the relation to the worker and, accordingly, the marriage certificate and birth certificate of the widow or widower must be submitted. Of course, a death certificate of the deceased worker is required.

The following questions deal with some of the other issues involved with applying for benefits. The timing of the application and the effect it may have on benefits, the advantages of a protective filing statement, and some issues that apply to business owners are also discussed.

Q **My husband is 67, soon to be 68, and is still working. He hasn't applied for his Social Security as of yet. What I was wondering is—if he applied now, would he get back pay to when he was 65 or to when he first applied?**

A His application for benefits can be retroactive for only six months from the date of filing.

☞**NOTE:** If he ever filed a *protective filing statement,* that would act as the filing date, even if he didn't file an application.

I recommend that everyone who is over 62 file a protective filing statement with Social Security periodically so as to make sure you collect all possible benefits.

Warning

Under a recent change in the law, there is no earnings limit if you are over full retirement age, so your husband should file his application immediately.

Q I will be 62 on March 5, 2008, and will file to collect Social Security. Because my birth date falls after 1937, will I have to wait an additional two years or does this only apply if you file at age 65? Thanks for your help.

A You can still collect at 62 (or more precisely, beginning with the month you will be age 62 "throughout the month"—in your case, April), but your benefit will be reduced an extra twelve months (not two). Because you were born in 1946, your *Full Retirement Age* is 66.

Q I have heard that the eligibility requirements have changed. I am 56 today and my birthday is in December. If I elect to take Social Security at age 62, what is the earliest date I can apply for benefits?

I also heard that only the last three years are being considered as eligible wages. How does that really work? Are the last three years of wages *averaged* and then that figure used as the income against which to calculate one's monthly Social Security check? Many thanks!

A You may apply three months before you turn 62. As a general rule, benefits are based on the highest thirty-five out of the last forty years of earnings and are *indexed* for inflation. Also, benefits are *actuarially reduced* (reduced for age) if received before *Full Retirement Age*—formerly age 65, but now gradually increasing in steps.

Q I will be 66 years old in the year 2009 and I am still working. If I choose to take a reduced rate for the period I am working, and work until I am 68 years of age, will I then be raised to the amount I would have received had I not received any money at age 66, or will I be frozen at the rate I received at 68 years of age? Would someone please answer this question, as I cannot receive an answer at our local Social Security office?

A There is no reduction of the benefit for you if you begin taking it at age 66. If you get a benefit for a month before you turn 66, there is a slight reduction for each such month, 5/9 of 1 percent (or 1/180) for each month of entitlement before *Full Retirement Age* (age 66 for you). The reduction factor for benefits before 66 may be eliminated after 66 if you did not get a full monthly benefit for such a month.

Additionally, you will get an increase for any month after age 66, up to age 70, that you do not get any benefits (provided you are insured for benefits). This is called the *delayed retirement credit*. For those turning 66 in 2009, it is ⅔ of 1% of your primary insurance amount (8% for a full year). You should go to your Social Security office immediately to file a *protective filing statement* and request an estimate of your benefit amount. Frequently, workers can get unexpected benefits, but it is crucial to protect your filing date.

Q I am considering retirement within the next six months from a full-time position I hold in the insurance field. I also own a small retail business with my business partner. How will the profits I earn from my business affect my Social Security benefits?

A Your earnings from a business, whether as wages or self-employment income, will affect your benefits just as any other earned income would, if you are under full retirement age. If you are under full retirement age, you lose $1 benefit for the calendar year for each $2 over the annual exempt amount. If you are over full retirement age, you lose $1 benefit for every $3 over the exempt amount. Additionally, exempt amounts are higher for the year you reach full retirement age. From that point on, earnings have no effect on benefits.

For 2007, the under-full retirement age annual exempt amount is $12,960; for those who reach full retirement age in 2007, it is $34,440. I don't know your age, but if you are under full retirement age, your application may have limits on how much retroactive benefits you may be able to pick up. Even if you are at full retirement age, there are limits on retroactivity, usually six months.

Many applicants would be able to get extra benefits they did not expect if they had filed sooner, or protected their filing dates. It is unfortunate to lose that money. I would suggest you file a "protective filing statement" as soon as possible. This may save you thousands of dollars.

Warning

When you own a business, Social Security will put your statements about your income and retirement allegations under a microscope. They will go on the assumption that you are lying to understate your income and they will request a detailed written statement from you. They will verify what you say by contacting customers and suppliers, and frequently pay surreptitious visits to your place of business, posing as a vendor or customer.

Q **May I sign up for Social Security by way of the Internet? Thanks.**

A Yes, you may apply for retirement, disability, and spouse's benefits online. Go to **www.ssa.gov/onlineservices**.

Q **I would like to know if I am eligible for widow's benefits. My husband just passed away last week. How do I find out and who do I contact? I am 63 years old.**

A It is important that you contact the local Social Security office as soon as possible because there are limitations on the retroactivity of your application—as little as one month, and possibly less. It is not necessary to wait for your husband's death certificate. It is important that you protect your filing date. You may submit your documents later. Social Security will give you the opportunity to obtain and submit documents after you have filed your application.

You can reach Social Security at 800-772-1213. They will tell you where your local Social Security office is. If you cannot get through to the number, you may also look in your local phone book under

"U.S. Government Offices." If you cannot do that, ask your post office for the nearest Social Security office, but DO NOT DELAY because you may lose benefits if you wait more than a month.

An application for a reduced widow's benefit may have no retroactivity. If you file it in the month after the month of your husband's death, it will have only one month's *retroactivity*, so do not delay.

Q My husband passed away seventeen months ago (age 66) at which time I sent the marriage certificate and received the *death benefit* of $255 (if I remember the sum correctly). I have not remarried and will be 60 soon. (I live in the state of Ohio.) Do I remember correctly that some benefits start for widows or widowers at age 60, as long as there has not been a remarriage? If a monthly check is granted, when I am 62 do I apply for my own (if larger)... or how long can I collect this widow's monthly? Thanks.

A Yes. The death benefit was $255, which was payable to a surviving spouse. You will be eligible for widow's benefits beginning at age 60, although they will be reduced because you are under *Full Retirement Age*. If you take the benefit at age 60, you will receive 71% of the full amount. If you remarry before age 60, you will not be entitled to the widow's benefit, but marriage after age 60 will not affect your benefits. If you are entitled to Social Security benefits on your own work account, you may be eligible beginning with age 62. If your own benefit amount is higher, you may switch over to your own. You may do this either at age 62 or at age 65.

It can be somewhat complicated to figure out your best advantage. It is a good idea to get benefit estimates from Social Security so you can work with the exact figures to calculate when would be the best time, if ever, to switch over to benefits on your own account. A person at the Social Security office would (or at least should) be glad to help you work through this.

Q I was born on January 1, 1943. When should I apply for Social Security? Thanks.

A Because your birthday is January 1, for Social Security purposes you attain your age on December 31, which means that you will be eligible for a benefit beginning with the month of January. Although you are technically age 62 as of December 31, you cannot collect the benefit for that month because you are not age 62 "throughout the month." However, because your "Social Security birthday" is the day before your birthday, you are considered to be born in 1942. The extra reduction months for you will be slightly less than they are for someone born in 1947. For those born in 1942, *Full Retirement Age* is age 65 and ten months, but for those born in 1941, *Full Retirement Age* is age 66. So your total reduction factor for your benefit at age 62 is slightly less than for those born in 1943.

Q I am turning 62 in August of this year. When do I need to apply for my Social Security since I am taking early retirement? I need to know if one needs a birth certificate to sign up for retirement.

A You should go to the Social Security office in May to apply for your retirement. Take your birth certificate and your W-2 forms for the last two years. If you are self-employed, take your tax returns.

✏**NOTE:** If you are self-employed and you are not closing your business outright or selling it to an unrelated party, you should be very careful before you go to Social Security. They will want you to establish—to their own satisfaction—that you are not continuing to work.

Q I was born in Germany. My father was in the U.S. Military Service at the time and my mother and father were stationed in Germany at the time of my birth. I only have a German (all written in German) birth certificate. Do I show this when I go to apply for my Social Security benefits? I am 54 now and just wanted to take care of any potential problems in the future, if this is a problem. I am an American citizen, of course, due to having been born to an American soldier's wife, but again, I have no proof of that. Is that a problem? I have worked since I was 17 and have always contributed to my Social Security through my paychecks.

A Social Security will be able to have your German birth certificate translated. Just make sure that you take the original certificate and not a photocopy when you go to the Social Security office. You do not have to worry about proving your citizenship because this is not a requirement to collect Social Security benefits. Social Security maintains a record of your earnings and there should be no problem with that.

Q I live in Citrus County and I will be 62 in June. What papers do I need and where do I go to sign up? Thank you.

A You go to your local Social Security office. You can obtain that location by calling the Social Security nationwide toll-free number at 800-772-1213. You will need your birth certificate, your Social Security number (you don't need the card but you should know the number), and it is a good idea to take your last two years' W-2 forms so that your current earnings can be added in to the calculation of your benefits right away.

Q I have a copy of your excellent book, *The Social Security Benefits Handbook*. There is a question I have but I could not find answered in your book and I would appreciate it if you would take the time to answer it.

I am self-employed and will be 64 this month. I am considering activating my Social Security. I need to estimate my net earnings for 2008. I will base this estimate on my 2007 net earnings given on my Schedule SE. There are two values given on this schedule. Do I use the higher or lower value? I am probably splitting hairs here as this is only an estimate. However, I would like to know the answer to this question for greater understanding and precision.

A Thank you for your comments regarding my other book, *The Social Security Benefits Handbook.*

The earnings test is based on all self-employment income (the higher figure on the Schedule SE). The lower figure is the net earnings from self-employment figure, which is used to calculate the Social Security tax. That figure is determined by applying a credit granted by a tax law passed in 1989. The Social Security rules make a distinction between net earnings from self-employment and self-employment income. Net earnings from self-employment is the figure after the tax credit deduction. The self-employment income is the net profit derived after business expenses. The amount used for the earnings test purposes under Social Security is the self-employment income figure, which would be the higher figure on the Schedule SE.

You should be very careful before you go to the Social Security office because you will be continuing your self-employment. Social Security will want to confirm that you are not understating your earnings so as to qualify for benefits. Because you are under *Full Retirement Age*, your earnings will affect the amount of your Social Security benefits payable. For this year when you are 64, you will lose $1 in Social Security benefits for every $2 over the annual exempt amount, which is $12,960 for 2007.

Be prepared to give a detailed explanation of your business and have your tax returns for the last several years available. If there is any substantial deviation between your earnings in pre-retirement years, Social Security will want an explanation. They may ask you for the names of your suppliers and major customers and they may ask you about your time spent at the business. They would like to pin you down to a schedule to see if you deviate from that. They sometimes send an investigator out to perform surveillance of your activities.

It is extremely important to have your ducks in order before going to the Social Security office. If the first interviewer believes that there is something suspicious or that you are being evasive or incomplete in your answers, he or she may flag your case for increased scrutiny. This is certainly a situation where first impressions count. Good luck.

Q In a discussion with a friend who will be turning 62, he stated that he needed to find his DD Form 214 so that he could get an additional bonus in his Social Security pay for serving in the military. I served in the military myself, but do not recall providing a copy of my DD Form 214 when I applied for Social Security benefits at age 62, over five years ago. Is there a bonus for serving in the military?

A Military service credits can be added to earnings for years before 1957. That is the year that military service became covered by Social Security. When calculating the benefit amount $160 is added to the annual earnings for each month of active duty. Because benefits are based on a worker's highest thirty-five years of earnings, it is now rare for the pre-1957 service to make a difference. If the military service will not result in an increase in the benefit, Social Security does not require proof of the service, as in your case. Your friend must have been working in noncovered employment after 1957, perhaps for a state or local government, so his military service made a difference in the calculation.

Q Can you move out of town without jeopardizing your benefits as long as it is accessible to the city within a certain time, that is, 1 to 1 1/2 hours travel time? What is the criteria?

A You can live anywhere you like and still receive your Social Security retirement benefits, with the exception of Cuba, North Korea, Cambodia, Vietnam, or certain other areas that were in the former Soviet Union. You will not have a problem no matter where you live within the United States, and in fact, most of the world.

Chapter 8

BENEFIT PAYMENTS

There are several different kinds of Social Security benefits and these benefits are calculated in various ways. The basic concept used to determine a Social Security benefit is the primary insurance amount. This is the amount that is used to calculate all benefits for the worker, as well as survivors and dependents. The primary insurance amount may be reduced if the benefit is taken before Full Retirement Age and it may be increased if retirement is delayed. Dependents in the case of a living worker will receive 50% of the worker's primary insurance amount. In the case of a deceased worker, the dependent's benefit is 75% of the primary insurance amount.

If the dependent is a spouse, widow, or widower under Full Retirement Age, then the benefit amount will be reduced for the age reduction. An exception to this is the case of the young widow (or widower) or young wife (or husband) whose entitlement is based on having a child under age 16 in her or his care.

In this chapter, we discuss questions that deal with the particulars of benefit amount calculations for the different types of beneficiaries and the different circumstances applying to each. We also discuss the effect of earnings on benefits and how the benefits can be reduced or suspended. This is generally referred to as work deductions.

The questions and answers in this chapter illustrate the different possibilities that are applicable to the several different types of Social Security benefits and the effect of age reductions and earnings reductions.

Q **There is a group called "Notches" that contacted my mother saying they were trying to regain money not being paid to people born between 1919 and 1927. Is this true?**

A The so-called "notch" issue has been exploited by several groups trying to raise some "big-time" money from donations for many years. Whatever you do, don't let Mom send any of her money! This has long been a dead issue that has already been looked into by Congress in the early 1990s.

In a nutshell, the concern arises because of a Carter era change in the law that adjusted the calculation of benefits to slow down large increases that arose due to a 1972 law that provided for automatic cost-of-living increases. The high inflation rates of the 1970s caused a windfall for those born after 1910, resulting in such high benefits that the financial integrity of the system was threatened. Congress provided for a recalculation of the way benefits are figured and phased it in over a transitional period for those born between 1917 and 1921.

Over time, benefit amounts again increased as younger workers reached retirement age. Their earnings subject to Social Security tax were higher, both because of inflation and because the maximum taxable earnings were increased to provide more tax revenue. For those born by 1927, the levels reached the pre-1917 level.

If you made a chart plotting benefit amounts over time by year of birth, those born before 1917 had higher benefits, 1918 babies' benefits dropped, and those born after 1921 had gradually rising benefits, thereby creating a "notch" effect, and giving rise to the term "notch babies."

This readjustment was a rational fix for the system. It did not deprive anyone of his or her money. Rather, it eliminated an overly generous system, relatively speaking. Don't forget, Social Security is a social insurance system, not some kind of annuity. Most benefici-aries, especially the older ones, including the "notch babies," have gotten more out of the system than they would have from a private annuity. That was, and continues to be, one of the problems for the financial integrity of the system.

Q How do they determine the amount of your Social Security checks? Is it based upon your three highest years or three last years?

A Social Security uses the highest thirty-five years. It indexes the earnings to account for inflation over the years, then determines an average monthly figure. Your benefit is based on a percentage of that. The percentage used is higher for lower average wages, and lower for higher average wages. The poor get more of a percentage of their average wages, and the rich get less, based on the idea that the poor need more than the rich.

For Example:
For the year 2009, a worker at age 65 with low annual earn-ings of $13,000 would receive an unreduced retirement benefit of $629 monthly ($7,548 annually), or about 58% of

annual earnings. A worker with high earnings of $100,000 would receive a monthly benefit of $1,940 monthly ($23,280 annually), or about 23%.

These numbers demonstrate that you should not count on Social Security as your sole source of retirement income. The program was never designed for that. It was designed to provide only about a third of retirement income, with the rest coming from private pensions and savings.

Q My husband has recently retired at age 58 because of cancer. He received a recent Social Security statement in which it summarizes correctly that he began work in 1972. It is not clear to us what his earned benefit will be at age 62 since he actually left the workforce prior to age 62. He has earned 144 credits over his life-time. Bottom line: What will his Social Security benefit be per month at age 62?

A First of all, he may be eligible for Social Security disability benefits if he cannot work. The amount would be the same as if he were at full retirement age. I would suggest you apply for them now and not wait till 62. The current maximum Social Security retirement benefit at full retirement age is approximately $1,998, plus another half of that for a wife of full retirement age. At age 62, the benefit is approximately 75% of the full retirement age benefit.

For those born between 1943 and 1954, such as your husband, there will be an additional twelve months of reduction, because for him *Full Retirement Age* will be age 66. The extra reduction months are calculated at 5/12 of 1 percent, in addition to the 20% reduction. For your husband it comes to 25% total. So, he would get about $1,490 at today's rates at age 62. But if he is approved for disability, he would get the unreduced amount of approximately $1,998. These figures are just approximations and assume maximum earnings.

Q What is the maximum monthly payment a retiree can receive from Social Security? What income is required for a retiree to qualify for the maximum monthly Social Security payment? Your answers will be greatly appreciated.

A The maximum retirement benefit for a wage earner turning 65 in 2007 is $1,998 per month. The current (2007) maximum earnings subject to FICA tax (the official name for the Social Security tax) is $97,500.

✏**NOTE:** The formula for computing the benefit includes thirty-five years. The maximum earnings have increased significantly over the last four decades. For example, the maximum FICA taxable earnings in 1960 was $4,800.

Q My husband received a Social Security statement of earnings. I haven't. Is this because I moved to Illinois five years ago? I work, so this would not make sense to me. What do I need to do?

A Social Security has a national program to mail earnings statements to all workers over age 25, but they do this gradually, based on your month of birth. You should get your statement about three months before your birthday. You may request it online at:

www.ssa.gov/mystatement/index.htm

Q **How would I go about finding out how much I have put toward my Social Security and how much the government or employers have matched me? Is there a form that you could send me?**

A In October 1999, the Social Security Administration began sending a Social Security statement automatically to workers age 25 or older who are not yet getting Social Security benefits. Your statement will arrive about three months before your birthday. In the future, you will get an updated statement about the same time each year. You can also request a statement at any time.

In your statement, you will see a year-by-year display of earnings that have been reported to your Social Security record. You will also find estimates of the benefits you and your family may be eligible for now and in the future.

You will receive a response to your statement request by U.S. mail in two to three weeks. The statement response will include: a complete earnings and Social Security tax history and estimates of retirement, survivors, and disability benefits. You may request a statement by calling or visiting your local Social Security office, by calling tollfree to 800-772-1213, or requesting it online at:

www.ssa.gov/mystatement/index.htm

Q I work for a financial institution and handle all accounts (checking, savings, and trust) for an elderly lady. She is having her Social Security deposited into her checking account at the present time. She has requested that I close her checking account and have her Social Security deposited into her savings account instead. How do I go about making these changes for our client? Please help.

A The client must call Social Security herself at 800-772-1213 and tell them to make the change to the new account. It is recommended that the old account not be closed out until you confirm that the direct deposits are going to the new account.

Q I have a friend who is 77 years of age and lives in the state of Utah. She recently was injured at work and may be able to receive a worker's compensation lump sum distribution. What will she owe in the way of taxes (federal, state, and Social Security) if she does receive the lump sum?

A Generally, workers' compensation awards are not taxable because they do not represent income. They are merely a replacement for something that has been lost. Receipt of these benefits do not affect Social Security retirement benefits, but may affect disability benefits if the combination of the two benefits (workers' compensation and disability) exceeds 80% of the average earnings. But your friend, being 77, is receiving retirement benefits.

Q I am 65 and have been collecting Social Security for three years. I have just started working. From my first paycheck they deducted FICA. Is this correct? If it is, will I get credit for money paid to Social Security?

A It is correct. Even though you are receiving Social Security benefits, any earnings you have are still subject to the Social Security and Medicare taxes. If the earnings in a retirement year are higher than the lowest earlier year used in the calculation of your benefit amount, then Social Security will replace the higher year's earnings with the lower year's earnings. This may have the effect of increasing your monthly benefit amount.

The Medicare portion of the tax will not increase any Medicare benefits because that is simply medical insurance. Because it may take a long time for Social Security to do a recalculation of your benefit, if your recent earnings are high, I would suggest you take your W-2 to the Social Security office as soon as you receive it and request a manual recalculation. Otherwise, it could take Social Security several years to get around to doing it.

Q I have worked and have Social Security benefits due to me at age 62 or 65. I have over forty quarters. I currently do not work. My husband is retired from the FBI. He told me that I will not be able to collect my Social Security benefits because he receives a federal pension. Is that true? And if so, why?

A It is not true that your husband's employment will have any effect on receipt of Social Security benefits on *your own work account*. You will get your own benefit based on your own earnings, regardless of your husband's employment. However, he may not be able to get spouse's benefit on your account, however, if he receives a federal pension because two-thirds of that pension. This is amount will be offset from any spouse's benefit that he could have received on your account.

Social Security law now is sex neutral so that a husband is eligible to receive spouse's benefits on his wife's work account if his own Social Security amount is less than that of the wife's. But because he is receiving a government pension, it is not likely that there would actually be anything payable due to the government pension offset. I think your husband got it a bit mixed up because it is he who cannot receive benefits on your account, not you.

Q **Can my wife get full benefits at age 62? If she has not worked much in the last fifteen years, is there a "ballpark" idea of what those might be?**

A Your wife may be eligible for benefits at age 62 on her own account if she has the required forty quarters of coverage. They do not have to be in the last fifteen years; they can be at any time. The amount of the benefit will be calculated based on the average indexed monthly earnings. At age 62, the benefits will be reduced because she is under *Full Retirement Age*. The amount of that reduction depends on her year of birth.

As far as a "ballpark" idea, I can tell you that an average monthly benefit at age 62 for workers with low earnings is about $600. For workers with average earnings, the monthly benefit would be about $975. A ballpark figure in your wife's case would be somewhere between those two figures because you say she has not worked much in the last fifteen years.

Of course, depending on her actual earnings record, it is possible that her monthly benefit could be even lower than the $600. You can get a written estimate of her benefit from the Social Security Administration.

Q I will be 62 in September and work full time. I was married for twenty-two years, divorced, and my ex-husband passed away in June 2007. My understanding is that I am entitled to receive survivor's benefits annually under his Social Security until I earn $17,500 per year. Since my annual salary exceeds this amount, is it possible for me to receive checks each year up until my year-to-date income reaches this amount? Thanks.

A You are potentially eligible to receive a widow's benefit as a surviving divorced wife on your ex-husband's account, assuming that you have not remarried before age 60. I think you have a misunderstanding as to the way your earnings affect Social Security benefits. I don't know where you got the $17,500 figure from (a few years ago the annual limit for those 65 and older was $17,000 per year, so maybe that is where you got it).

The way your earnings affect your Social Security benefits is determined by the total annual earnings in a given year for earnings before you attain *Full Retirement Age*. For those such as yourself, below *Full Retirement Age* in the year 2007, the annual exempt amount is $12,960. If your annual earnings do not exceed that amount, then you may collect all the year's Social Security benefits. If your annual earnings do exceed that amount, then you lose $1 in Social Security benefits for every $2 of earnings over that amount.

You say you earn more than $17,500 a year. If, for example, you earned $27,500, that would be $14,540 excess, which would require $7,270 to be withheld from any Social Security benefits to which you would otherwise be entitled. If the total Social Security benefits for the year exceed $7,270, then you may receive the balance.

Because I do not know what your benefit amount would be, nor do I know what your annual earnings are, I cannot tell you if you could receive benefits for the year 2007. However, because you will be 62, you should get a benefit estimate from the Social Security office to find out if you may be able to receive some benefits even while you are working.

✐**NOTE:** You may be eligible for benefits on your own account, as well as on your ex-husband's account. You also have the option of taking reduced benefits on the one account and waiting until you reach *Full Retirement Age* to take an unreduced benefit on the other account. To make this decision, it is important to get benefit estimates on both accounts.

The personnel at the Social Security office are required to work through these various options with you. Because this is rather complicated, if you do not feel comfortable with the interviewer at Social Security, you may ask to speak to a supervisor.

Q I currently draw Social Security due to my husband passing away four years ago. My daughter also collects Social Security. As for me, I have started to work fulltime and want to know how this will affect my part of the Social Security that I draw. Isn't there a formula that I figure? Do I just save what I have to pay back or do they start deducting it every month? Thanks.

A If you are under *Full Retirement Age*, then your earnings will effect the benefits you receive for yourself. I am assuming that you are a young widow because you have a child who is also collecting on the account. The amount you can earn in 2007 with no affect on your benefits is $12,960. If you earn over that amount, then you will lose $1 in Social Security benefits for every $2 over that limit. You must report to Social Security if you expect your annual earnings to exceed this exempt amount. They will withhold your benefits based on that estimate. After you receive your actual earnings for the year, you can file an annual report with Social Security. These amounts can be adjusted. If you want to avoid having to pay back money to Social Security after the annual report, then you should be as accurate as possible in giving your estimate of earnings for the year.

Q I would like to know why they have never increased the amount Social Security gives you when your loved one dies. With the cost for burial, it is a terrible burden on a person with a fixed income. Why don't they give the last check the deceased person was to receive?

A The lump sum death benefit of $255 has not been changed in at least the last thirty years. This is a matter of law for the Congress to decide. I agree that $255 hardly seems adequate. In fact, Congress has restricted the availability of the lump sum death payment to go only to surviving widows or widowers and not to other family members or other persons, even those paying the funeral bill.

Concerning your comment about the last check that a deceased was supposed to receive, it is not payable because Social Security benefits terminate with the month of death and the benefit checks are paid in *arrears.* The check received in a given month is actually payment for the prior month. Accordingly, it is not payable because of the termination of entitlement.

Q **I am presently working parttime and contributing to Social Security and Medicare. My question is: Am I entitled to an increase in my monthly benefits? If so, how is it calculated? Thank you for your time.**

A You may be entitled to an increase in your monthly benefits if your current earnings are higher than the lowest year's earnings used in the calculation of your benefits. Generally speaking, thirty-five years are used to calculate a Social Security benefit. One of those years in the distant past may indeed be lower than your current earnings. If not, then there will be no increase in your monthly benefits.

Because you are working parttime, I would not expect an increase. If there is one, it will be minimal, perhaps just a few dollars. It is calculated automatically by Social Security when the earnings are posted to the earnings record. Social Security then compares that to their beneficiary rolls.

This process usually takes several years, so if you want to expedite any possible recalculation, take your W-2 form or other evidence of earnings to the Social Security office to request a manual recalculation. If done manually, it would take a matter of just a few months, rather than a few years.

Q I am 54 years old and want to know my Social Security benefits at 62 and 65 years old. Once I came across (online) a software application, which based on yearly income and retirement age, calculates Social Security benefits. Can you please advise me of the website, if, of course, it still exists? Thank you very much.

A The Social Security Administration has an extensive website at **www.ssa.gov** where you will find a benefits calculator link that you can access. In general terms, I can give you the average amounts of retirement benefits for workers with high earnings and maximum earnings over the course of their work life.

For workers with maximum earnings in the year 2007, the benefit at age 62 is $1,598 per month, and at age 65 it is $1,998 per month. Of course, these are only approximations, but it gives you an idea of the benefit amounts for workers with maximum earnings.

Q My husband is going to retire in one year and has had an aortic valve replacement. He is currently 57 years old. We were told that he would qualify for full Social Security upon his retirement. Is this true? Thank you for your assistance.

A It does not sound true, unless he is totally disabled. The Social Security benefit is paid fully at *Full Retirement Age*, which is set by law and depends on your year of birth. Your husband, being 57 years old in 2007, would have been born in 1950. For persons born from 1943 to 1954, the *Full Retirement Age* is age 66. Any Social Security benefits received prior to that time will be reduced. At age 62, that reduction would come out to a 25% reduction of the full benefit.

However, if your husband qualifies for Social Security disability benefits, then for calculation of benefit purposes, his amount will be the same as if he had turned 66 in the year he becomes disabled.

Additionally, when disability benefits are granted, this results in a freeze on the earnings record for calculation purposes. Perhaps that is what you were thinking of. I would suggest that he consider filing for the Social Security disability even though he is retiring. The real question is whether or not he is physically able to continue working. There are many advantages to being entitled to Social Security disability, including entitlement to Medicare coverage after twenty-four months of entitlement to the disability benefit. I wish you and your husband the best of luck with this.

Q Can I, as a female and at the age of 62, receive Social Security and severance pay at the same time?

A Yes. You, as a female and at the age of 62, may receive Social Security and severance pay at the same time. Your sex has nothing to do with the issue because Social Security is now sex-neutral. At age 62, if you are receiving Social Security retirement benefits, your earnings, if over the annual exempt amount, will cause a reduction of $1 of Social Security benefits for every $2 over the exempt limit.

Severance pay, which is received as a payment made upon termination of employment because of retirement, is not considered earnings for the earnings test purposes, although it may be subject to Social Security tax. Therefore, the severance pay will not affect the amount of Social Security benefits that you may receive.

Q I would like to know if your ex-wife of ten or more years gets a part of your Social Security. Does that mean your monthly amount decreases?

A No. The entitlement of an ex-wife has no effect on your benefit or anyone else in your family receiving on your account. She may receive an ex-wife's benefit on your account, but the other benefits payable on the account will not be reduced.

Q I will soon retire at the age of 55. Will I be penalized when filing for Social Security at age 62? Example: On the statement from the Social Security Administration, it states at the age of 62 I will draw $1,230 a month. If I retire from work at age 55, will I still draw $1,230 at the age of 62 when I sign up on Social Security?

A You must look carefully at the statement. Many times these estimates assume that you will continue to earn wages in a proportionate amount as your prior earnings up until the time you apply for Social Security. In your case, if the figure of $1,230 per month was based on that assumption of continued earnings, then the actual benefit amount will be lower at 62 because you will have approximately seven years of zero earnings.

The benefit amount is calculated based on average indexed monthly earnings over thirty-five years. Usually the last years are the highest years, so it probably will have an effect on your benefit amount if you retire at the age of 55. You can ask Social Security to refigure your benefit estimate based on the assumption of no earnings after age 55 to get a more accurate figure.

Q What is the maximum amount for Social Security payment for 2007?

A It depends what you are talking about. The maximum Social Security monthly benefit amount for a retired worker at age 65 is approximately $1,998. For twelve months this would result in $23,976. If a wife is entitled on the account, it is possible that another 50% of that figure would be added.

you are talking about the annual earnings that are subject to the Social Security tax, then the amount for 2007 is $97,500 for the Social Security portion (6.2% for the employer and 6.2% for the employee). The Medicare portion (1.45% for the employer and 1.45% for the employee) is not limited and is paid on the full actual earnings.

If you are referring to the earnings limitation for benefit purposes, then for persons attaining *Full Retirement Age* in 2007, the exempt amount of earnings is $34,400 per year. For those under *Full Retirement Age*, the annual exempt amount is $12,960 per year.

Q I understand that I can take 37.5% of my ex-husband's Social Security when I turn 62 and 50% when I turn 65. I was married for more than the ten-year limit. Now I am curious as to how I can find out how much I would receive at the 62 age level and the 65 age level. I need that information to make my decision of which year to retire.

A You must find out the actual dollar amount from Social Security. You will need to identify your ex-husband. If you do not have his Social Security number, you will need his date of birth, full name, and other personal information so that they may obtain the record. You may request that benefit estimate from Social Security on his record. It will take them a few months to get the information to you.

Q I am writing to find out how my father's monthly checks will be affected because he was forced to sell his share of the company stock that he worked for. My father was forced to retire because he had lung cancer and later brain cancer, all within two years. He was told by the doctors that he will never drive a motor vehicle again. Since this was his livelihood, he had to retire. Will this affect his monthly Social Security checks? Thank you.

A It depends on how old your father is. If he is over 65, then there will be no effect on his benefits. If he is under 65, then his retirement benefit will be less if he has years with zero earnings. Social Security uses the average indexed monthly earnings over a period of thirty-five years to calculate the benefits.

Your father should apply for Social Security disability because that will put a freeze on his earnings record. For calculation of benefit purposes, it will be the same as if he turned 65 (or *Full Retirement Age*) in the year he becomes disabled.

Q My sister is 65 and on Social Security. Recently her husband retired and is now also drawing Social Security. Because her husband made too much money before he retired, she is not receiving a check for the month of March. Why are they penalizing her instead of him? What do his wages have to do with her Social Security check? Your answer will be greatly appreciated. Thank you.

A Under the Social Security law, the earnings of a worker affect all beneficiaries receiving benefits on his account if he goes over the annual limit. If the wife receives on her own earnings record, then the husband's earnings will not affect those benefits. It is because she receives some or all of her Social Security benefits based on her entitlement as a wife that his earnings affect her benefits.

Q Could you please advise how we can get one of the direct deposit forms for my mother-in-law's Social Security check? We have never been able to convince her to do direct deposit, but now she is getting to the point where she cannot get out to cash her check. Is there a form on the Internet that we can print off or does the bank have some? I will appreciate your reply.

A You can get the form either at the bank or from the Internet. The bank will be glad to make arrangements to have your Social Security money directly deposited into the account and you might as well let them do the work. They will certainly benefit from your business. If you prefer, you can request the form from the Social Security Administration at 800-772-1213. You may download the form online at:

www.ssa.gov/deposit/

Q My father-in-law is getting Social Security and is 79 years old. He asked me to look into his account and see what he should be receiving at this age. He says his brother and sister are getting more than he is. Is there a way we can find out what he should be getting? He is Spanish and speaks very little English. Thank you.

A At 79 years old I assume that your father-in-law has been receiving Social Security for ten or fifteen years at least. When he was first entitled to Social Security, he received an award letter stating the amount of his benefit. Each year after that he received a cost of living adjustment. If he has worked after first becoming entitled, any additional earnings, if higher than earlier years used in the calculation of his benefit, would also go to increase his benefit amount.

You may go to the local Social Security office with him and ask for an explanation of the calculation of his benefits. The Social Security personnel should be able to obtain his earnings record and show you on paper how many years were used and what the earnings were for those years.

It is very possible, and in fact likely, that his brother and sister are receiving different amounts because each benefit is calculated based on the particular earnings record of each worker. If his brother and sister earned more than he did, then their benefits would be higher. Additionally, it is possible that two people with the same amount of earnings could receive different benefit amounts depending on their different years of birth.

Over the years, Social Security has adjusted the calculation of benefits to take into account several factors, including the long-term financial viability of the program, and as a result, benefit amounts can vary. But if you go to the Social Security office, you should receive a satisfactory answer. You will have to bring your father-in-law with you because Social Security is prohibited from disclosing to third persons information about a beneficiary unless you have been appointed as his representative. The easiest thing is simply to take your father-in-law with you to the Social Security office.

Q My husband turned 62 on January 7. We filed for Social Security. My question is: We didn't receive our first check until March 13th. Isn't he eligible as of January 7? It appears to me that he was not paid for January and February, or was March the soonest they could start payment?

A There are no benefits payable to your husband for January because he was not 62 throughout the entire month. Under a change in the Social Security law a few years ago, a new requirement was added to provide that no benefit is payable for the month you turn 62. You must be age 62 throughout the entire month, so your husband's first month of entitlement is actually February. Social Security pays the benefit checks in *arrears*, so that the February payment is not due until March, which is when it was paid.

Q What is the maximum dollar amount that Social Security pays?

A For a retiree turning 65 in 2007, the maximum amount is $1,998 per month. If the worker is married, a wife may receive up to one-half of that amount on his account.

Q Recently my great aunt passed away. Her brother was living with her and has recently moved in with my aunt. Since then, he has not received his Social Security checks. How do I get an address change put through and replacement checks? Is there a phone number that I can call?

A Social Security has a toll-free number nationwide, which is 800-772-1213. Additionally, you can contact your local Social Security office in person or by mail. To find your nearest Social Security office, look in the blue pages section of your phone book directory under "U.S. Government" or you can ask at your local post office for the address of the nearest Social Security office.

Q I can't find a job even on a part-time basis. I am one credit away from having my forty quarters that is needed to qualify for Social Security. Is there anything that can be done about this situation?

A The only thing that can be done is for you to obtain covered employment for one more quarter. If you do not have the forty quarters of coverage, you will not be eligible for the retirement benefit. For calendar year 2007, you must earn $1,000 for each quarter of coverage.

Q I live in the state of Rhode Island and I have a mother-in-law who collects Social Security. About six or eight months ago, she collected $20,000 from her ex-husband's death and never claimed it. She instead hid the money in her son's name and has been on a spending spree ever since. Is there a fraud department within the Social Security division that can be contacted?

A I am not sure what fraud you suspect she has committed. She may collect Social Security as well as receive a death benefit from an ex-husband's account. Why do you suspect that she has committed a fraud against the Social Security Administration? If she is receiving Supplemental Security Income, which is a needs-based program, then that may very well be a fraud. But if she is receiving regular Social Security, her receipt of a death benefit from some other source will not affect her benefit.

I would check a little more carefully before making accusations against your mother-in-law, but if you sincerely believe that there is some fraud going on, you may report it to the Social Security Administration by calling 800-269-0271. Before you do that you should have your facts and details together because they will be asking you some specific questions.

Q I have a question about a five-year-old receiving Social Security from the death of her father, but her mother uses the money for her own use. What I would like to know is, is she supposed to use that money for the baby and put some of it in a trust fund for her?

A The payee of a Social Security beneficiary, even if it is the mother, is responsible to use the funds for the needs of the child. This may include food, clothing, shelter, and medical expenses. If there is any money left over from these uses, then it should be saved in an insured account for the benefit of the child. If the money is insufficient to leave any savings, then the entire amount may be used for the benefit of the child.

If you suspect that there is misuse of the money, you can, of course, report that to the Social Security Administration. However, in the case of a natural mother with the child in the house, it is perfectly proper to apply the Social Security benefits to the operating costs of the household where the child lives, especially where the amount of the Social Security benefit is modest.

Of course, the application of the Social Security benefits for a portion of the household expenses must be based on a reasonable portion representing the child's share of the household expenses. Even if there is a somewhat disproportionate contribution of the child's benefits to the household, this may also be justified if it contributes to the overall well-being and stability of the family unit because the child benefits from such a stable household.

Q **I would like to know about rent subsidy and how it works and who is entitled to it. Thank you.**

A Social Security does not provide any rent subsidies. Social Security benefits are cash benefits only, plus Medicare, which provides hospital and medical insurance. There are other Federal programs that provide housing subsidies for the needy, but it is not from the Social Security Administration.

I would suggest you contact the federal department of Housing and Urban Development.

U.S. Department of Housing and Urban Development
451 7th Street South West
Washington, DC 20410
202-708-1112

Q How do I make my son qualify for Social Security or what do I need for him to claim Social Security?

A He must work and earn sufficient quarters in order to be eligible for Social Security benefits on his own account. If he is a minor child of a retired, disabled, or deceased worker who had enough quarters of coverage, he may be eligible for a child's benefit. If he is disabled before age 22, he may also be eligible as a disabled adult child if he is the child of an insured worker who is entitled to retirement or disability benefits or who is deceased.

If you believe your son may be eligible for benefits as a child, then you should go to your Social Security office without delay and file a protective filing statement and inquire about possible benefits. Take with you any information pertaining to the parent of the child on whose account you may be eligible. Best wishes.

Q My father passed away in September. I am an only child. I am married and since my mother is disabled she is living with me now. I manage her money. She is 85 years old and receives a Social Security check of $969. It was raised to what my Dad was receiving when he passed away. My question is does she have to file an income tax return? This is her only income except for a statement where my father had won $700 playing bingo. Thanks in advance for your help.

A Social Security benefits are not taxable unless your total income is over $25,000 for an individual, or $32,000 for married couples. Because your mother's only income is less than these limits, even with the bingo earnings, it would not appear that any tax is due on the benefits.

Q I would like to get a statement of my up-to-date earnings reported to Social Security. I plan to retire in about five years and would like to know about how much I will be able to receive.

A You can call the Social Security Administration at 800-772-1213 to request a Social Security Statement. You can also go online to the Social Security Administration page that has online calculators so you can get your own estimate. That page is at: **www.ssa.gov/planners/calculators.htm**. Online services are available Monday through Friday from 6:00 a.m. to 1:00 a.m., on Saturday from 8:00 a.m. to 11:00 p.m., and on Sunday from 8:00 a.m. to 8:00 p.m.

Of course, you can also visit your local Social Security office during business hours. (This is not a desirable thing to do unless you are in a very small town.) Or, write to the local office. There is an online office locator at **www.ssa.gov/locator** where you put in your zip code and you get the address and a map with directions.

Q Is there any way of having income tax withheld from Social Security? My husband is still working, as well as collecting, and this places a burden on us at tax time. Thank you for a response.

A If you really want to let the government use your money interest-free before you have to give it to them, you can complete IRS Form W-4V (Voluntary Withholding Request). You can choose what percentage you want withheld, either 7%, 10%, 15%, or 27%. You cannot choose any other percentage amount, or even a flat rate. Return the form to your local Social Security office.

Q I would like to get some information regarding Supplemental Security Income. How do you become eligible and what is the criteria?

A *Supplemental Security Income*, also known as SSI, is often confused with Social Security, but it is a completely different program. Part of the confusion arises from the fact that the Social Security Administration is the federal agency that administers both.

Supplemental Security Income is a federal welfare program that came into effect almost thirty years ago. It was designed to provide a minimum amount of income to individuals regardless of their work and earnings under Social Security.

There is no quarter of coverage requirement or other earnings requirement to collect the benefit. However, because it is a needs-based program, the recipient's income—whether it is earned or unearned—will effect the eligibility. Additionally, assets over certain amounts will make a person ineligible, but not all assets count. Supplemental Security Income is designed for the aged, blind, or disabled persons of limited needs. The amount of the monthly payment depends on the living arrangement of the recipient.

Generally speaking, if the individual's assets are greater than $2,000 (not counting a residence or a vehicle), then the person will not be eligible for Supplemental Security Income. For a couple, that figure is $3,000. The federal payment rates are very modest. For an individual in the year 2007, that figure is $623 per month. Income from other sources may be deducted from that amount.

The Supplemental Security Income program is very complex. The payments can vary greatly depending on the type of income, the number of people living in the household, and the type of assets owned by the individual. Additionally, several of the states supplement federal benefit amounts and have their own requirements as to living arrangements and other criteria.

Q My father has a quick question regarding Supplemental Security Income. Can he collect unemployment while he is on Supplemental Security Income? Thank you.

A Supplemental Security Income is a needs-based federal program administered by Social Security Administration. All income is taken into account and affects the Supplemental Security Income benefit. He may be entitled to collect both, but if the unemployment is more than the Supplemental Security Income, the Supplemental Security Income will be suspended or reduced while he collects the unemployment.

Chapter 9

PAYING SOCIAL SECURITY TAX

Social Security benefits and Medicare are funded by FICA taxes on the earnings of workers in covered employment. The total tax rate is 15.3%. If you are an employee, half of that amount is paid by the employer, and the other half is deducted from your paycheck. If you are self-employed, you must pay the entire 15.3% yourself. The maximum earnings subject to the Social Security portion tax is $97,500 per annum. The Social Security portion of the payroll tax is 12.4%. The remainder is the Medicare portion (2.9%) and is deducted from total earnings without limit. One-half (1.45%) is paid by the employer and the other half by the employee.

When you receive Social Security benefits, you may have to pay an income tax on a portion of the benefits. If you file as a single taxpayer, and your total income, including nontaxable income from other sources, exceeds $25,000 per annum, then you must pay income tax on 50% of the Social Security benefits in excess of $25,000 of your total income. If the Social Security benefits are in excess of $34,000 of total income, then you must pay taxes on 85% of your Social Security benefits. For a couple, the figures are higher—$32,000 for the threshold amount; $32,000 for the 50% excess level and $44,000 for the 85% excess level.

If you are working and receiving Social Security benefits, you must pay taxes on your earnings as well as income taxes on your Social Security benefits if they exceed these levels.

Q Could you please tell me what the maximum salary that Social Security benefits are paid on for the year 2006 and for the year 2007 also? Thank you for your attention to this question.

A The maximum earnings subject to the FICA tax (the Social Security tax) are $94,200 in 2006 and $97,500 in 2007.

☞**NOTE:** The Medicare portion (1.45%) has no limit. The maximum benefit per month for workers turning 65 in 2007 is $1,998 per month.

Q I was contacted by one of our former employees stating that his Social Security number was wrong on his W-2. He is concerned that the Social Security withholding will not be applied to his account. What do I need to do to correct this error? He is no longer employed by us and I have already submitted all my forms to the IRS.

A You must file an amended payroll tax return with the IRS to correct the number. You should indicate on the form that it is a "corrected" form. Additionally, you can re-issue a W-2 with the correct Social Security number to your former employee and indicate on the form that it is "corrected as to SSN." That way the ex-employee will have a record of the earnings. You may also advise the ex-employee to check with Social Security in a couple of years to make sure that his record has been corrected.

It is a good idea in general for all employees to check their Social Security wage records with Social Security every three years because mistakes happen all the time. There are revised forms for correcting the W-2 and W-3 Forms (the W-3 form is the one you use to transmit the W-2 information to the government).

Form W-2c and Form W-3c are used to submit corrections to the Social Security Administration. You can order these forms as well as additional instructions by calling 800-829-3676. You should not use the forms from the IRS to make this correction with Social Security.

Q **Please let me know if there are any changes to the Social Security tax rates for 2007.**

A The tax rates remain the same at 7.65% for an employee matched by the employer and 15.30% for the self-employed person. The Medicare portion is 1.45% (2.9% for the self-employed). The maximum earnings taxable has increased for Social Security purposes and in the year 2007 is now $97,500. However, there is no limit on the amount of earnings subject to the Medicare tax.

Q **I worked for the Department of Defense in 1993 full time. My wife also worked there. When we received our report of earnings from Social Security, it showed we put no money into Social Security. We both filed taxes that year and were not married at that time. What should I do because the base is now closed? This will affect my Social Security input and is important.**

A Generally speaking, there is a statute of limitations on correcting earnings records. This statute of limitations is three years, two months, and fifteen days after the year in which the wages were paid. However, an exception may be found where you have filed a tax return and reported the earnings before the end of the time limitation. So you should be able to correct your earnings record by taking your tax returns to the Social Security administration and asking them to correct their records to reflect the actual earnings.

Q **My husband's employer wants to change his pay and not take any taxes or Social Security out. I understand that we will have to pay taxes on his wages come tax time, but how does that affect Social Security? Will we have to pay into that too or will it just look like he never worked during the time he is with this company? Does an employer have to pay into Social Security for employees? Thanks.**

A Yes. An employer is required by law to contribute not only the deductions from the employee's pay, but also to match the Social Security tax so that the employer pays half of the overall FICA tax. The amount of that overall tax including Medicare is 15.3%. If you are an employee, your employer pays 7.65% and you pay 7.65%.

What the employer is trying to do here is avoid that legal obligation and shift it over to you. If your husband is, in fact, an *employee*, as opposed to an *independent contractor*, then what the employer is attempting to do here is illegal. An employee is one who is under the control of the employer as to the time hours, means, and methods of work. An independent contractor sets his own rules and usually provides his own tools, equipment and materials.

Many employers try to say that their employees are really independent contractors so that they can avoid not only the FICA tax, but also workers' compensation, disability benefits, unemployment compensation, taxes, and other obligations that employers have.

Presumably your husband is afraid to lose his job. However, it may be a good idea to look for other employment. If the employer fails to withhold and pay the proper taxes from your husband's earnings, you may request Social Security to correct the earnings record, but you must do that timely and you will need facts, evidence, and proof of the actual relationship. If Social Security determines that the relationship is one of employer/employee, rather than independent contractor, then they can make that determination and report it to the IRS who will collect the taxes from the employer and credit your husband's payroll. However, it certainly seems like a messy situation.

Q **Is there a maximum amount of money you pay every year on your Social Security contributions? I have a friend that recently got a refund from the Social Security services offices because he was informed that they collected too much from him for that year and so they are refunding him his excess payment. I am single and 31 years old. My mom is still working and she is 59 years old.**

A The maximum earnings that are subject to Social Security tax for the year 2007 is $97,500. If you have more than one employer, it is possible that the employers combined withheld more than they should have and that his why your friend is receiving a refund.

There is no limit on the Medicare portion of the Social Security taxes. The Medicare portion of the tax rate is 2.9% on all earnings. Half of this is paid by the employer and half is paid by the employee. If you are self-employed, you pay the entire portion yourself.

Q **I am a Louisiana resident and I have two questions.**

1.   **What is the minimum salary within a given year that a person must earn and pay Social Security on to qualify as an official quarter/year of contribution or is there a minimum at all?**

2.   **I am an ordained minister and I am currently Social Security exempt. However, I have a sideline business unrelated to my ministry work and it is set up as an S Corporation. Can I begin to pay Social Security taxes on my business wages and not on my ministering wages? I do not have forty quarters, therefore, I want to begin to pay Social Security on just the business wages. If so, how do I go about getting it done?**

A You must earn $1,000 of wages in 2007 to get credit for one quarter of coverage. For a calendar year, you must earn four times that to get credit for the full four quarters. However, you cannot be credited for a future quarter even if your earnings in the first part of the year exceed the annual amount. If your annual earnings for the year are at least $4,000, you will be entitled to four quarters for that year. Although, as I just noted, you cannot be credited with a quarter until it actually arrives in time. Otherwise, it does not matter when you make the earnings so long as the annual amount is earned you can receive the four quarters for the given year.

In your case, you can earn Social Security credits for employment unrelated to your exempt ministry work. In order to get the credits, you must file a tax return that identifies you as earning wages. Because your business is structured as an S Corporation and the profits are distributed to you as dividends, you may have to make some adjustments on the form of your business. I would suggest you consult with your accountant to make sure that your S Corporation earnings and distributions are reported as wages to the Social Security Administration for purposes of getting the Social Security credits.

In the normal case, an employer reports wages to Social Security or if a person is self-employed, the Schedule C attachment to the tax return reports the net earnings from self-employment, which IRS transmits to the Social Security Administration. It is permissible to earn Social Security credit for work covered by Social Security even though you may also have employment in noncovered employment. Of course, you will only receive Social Security benefits based on the Social Security covered employment.

Q **How does a person pay the Social Security tax if he earns income that is not reported on a W2 form, but is reported on a 1099-MISC form?**

A Income earned as so-called "1099 income" may be self-employment income, in which case you should complete a Schedule C with your tax return. You will have to pay your own taxes on this income. Frequently, an employer, to avoid paying the FICA payroll tax and other costs such as workers' compensation and disability insurance, will give a worker the 1099 instead of the W-2. If you are really an employee and not self-employed, you can ask Social Security to correct your earnings record by making a determination of your status.

Q **How would a person go about being removed from the Social Security system? Could you send me information on how or where I could find this information?**

A Although the Social Security taxes (FICA) on earnings are called "contributions" by the law and regulations, there is nothing voluntary about them. If they are not paid, the IRS will sue, levy, seize and maybe even incarcerate you. It is up to Congress to change the law.

Chapter 10

THE SOCIAL SECURITY CARD, NUMBER, AND IDENTITY THEFT

A Social Security number is assigned to record each individual's earnings and monitor benefits paid under the Social Security program. These numbers are commonly used by businesses for identification purposes. Social Security has no responsibility or control over the disclosure of the Social Security number once you give it to a third party. It is not necessary to have the physical card in your possession if you know the number.

To get a number assigned, an in-person interview at the Social Security office is mandatory if the applicant is age 18 or older. If the individual is unable to go to the office, Social Security can arrange for a home visit. You will need evidence of you age, identity, and citizenship. If you are merely obtaining a duplicate card, you only need show proof of identity.

Because Social Security numbers are so commonly used by businesses, it is easy to impersonate someone by use of the number. There has been a significant increase in recent years of what is referred to as "identity theft." Thieves have used Social Security numbers to obtain fraudulent credit cards and perpetrate other financial fraud. If you have suffered a disadvantage because someone has used your Social Security number, you may request a new number. You must convince Social Security that you have done everything you can to fix the problem before they will assign a new number. Social Security will not assign a new number if you want one to avoid legal responsibility, avoid a poor credit record, or file for bankruptcy.

Q I have reason to believe that someone may have gotten hold of my Social Security number and may be using it to get credit cards, loans, etc. How can I check to see if this has really happened?

A You may contact the Social Security fraud hotline at 800-269-0271. You may also contact the Federal Trade Commission ID Theft Hotline at 877-438-4338.

Q Is it OK to laminate a Social Security card?

A While it is not illegal to laminate your card, the Social Security Administration advises against it. If a card is laminated, it may be impossible to detect important security features that protect against counterfeit cards.

Q I would like to know where I can request a corporate Social Security number for my business. Please let me know.

A There is no such thing as a corporate Social Security number. Social Security numbers are only assigned to individuals. You may be referring to an employer's identification number, which is a number assigned by the Internal Revenue Service for employers whether they be self-employed or corporations. I would suggest that you contact the Internal Revenue Service for that application form if that is what you are referring to.

Q I presently work for a major energy company and the company uses a number of computer programs. One such program has hundreds of employees' Social Security numbers in plain view. In the spirit of identity theft is this a safe practice? Is the company allowed to publicly display an employee's Social Security number? What recourse do the employees have? This matter has been brought to the attention of management and nothing has been done to resolve it.

A There is no restriction on an employer's or anyone's use of a Social Security number so long as it is not for a fraudulent purpose. Yes, it does create a danger of identity theft, but there is nothing you can do to prevent that. If, however, you think that someone has stolen another's identity, you can report it both to the Social Security Administration as well as to the Federal Trade Commission. The Social Security fraud hotline number is 800-269-0271. The Federal Trade Commission ID Theft Hotline is 877-438-4338.

Q What is the quickest way that I can get a replacement Social Security card? Thanks.

A The quickest way is to go to the Social Security office with proof of your identity. For a replacement card you can use your driver's license; state-issued, non-driver identity card; or, a United States passport. There are many other forms of identification that Social Security will accept if you already have a number and just need a replacement.

QI need to know how I can obtain a Social Security number if both parents of the minor are locked up in prison and he is too young to get it himself.

APresumably, the minor will have a guardian appointed. If not, one should be. The guardian may apply for the Social Security number.

QI am currently in the eighth grade and I live in the state of California. I have a homework assignment from my history teacher. One of the questions that is part of my assignment is "when did our country start giving out the social securities to people?"

AThe Social Security Act was passed into law on August 14, 1935. It became effective for payroll deductions in 1937, at which time the first Social Security benefits where paid to retirees. In 1939, the law was broadened to include dependents and survivors. In the 1950s, disability benefits were added, as well as coverage for self-employed individuals. The program has come to encompass almost all workers in America. Currently, there are almost 46 million beneficiaries who receive Social Security benefits each year.

QCan you find out someone's age or date of birth through their Social Security card? Thank you for your anticipated response.

A Social Security maintains the information of each person's date of birth when a Social Security number is applied for. Social Security is not permitted to disclose this information. However, many private companies such as banks and credit card companies obtain date of birth and Social Security information. There are many sources in the private sector to obtain private information about someone based on their Social Security number.

Q **I need verification as to the law regarding who can legally ask for my Social Security number and who does not have the right to do so. Can you tell me specifically who has the right to do so and exactly what the law says? If you could, I would appreciate the exact law title and such. Thank you very much.**

A Social Security numbers are authorized for use by the Social Security Administration in administering the Social Security program. Additionally, certain third parties are authorized to use Social Security numbers for specific purposes including the Internal Revenue Service, the Department of Treasury, banks, state governments, the parent locator service, and various other federal agencies. Many private companies have used and continue to use the Social Security number for their own purposes. Although this is not authorized by Social Security, these uses are not illegal. Social Security has no authority to prevent the use of Social Security numbers.

According to the Social Security programs operations manual, there is no law that prevents a third party from using or requesting a Social Security number as an identifier. Of course, an individual can refuse to furnish the Social Security number as requested, but the third party can also refuse to issue the benefit or service in the event of such refusal. Because there is no law that prohibits the use of the numbers, it is difficult to cite such a law. However, I can direct your attention to the Social Security Programs Operations Manual, Section RM00201.010, entitled "Nonprogram Use of the Social Security Number."

Q My 401(k) plan administrator informed me that if there was ever incorrect information on my Social Security record, I have only three years to find and correct the problem. Basically, what he is telling me, is that it is up to me personally to check my record periodically for mistakes or possible fraud. If I don't fix it within three years, it will remain on my record. Is this statement true?

I had my Social Security card stolen about one year ago, and although I reported it stolen, it seems that this "three- year" law could pose potential problems in the future.

A Your administrator has correctly stated the general rule (almost—it is three years, three months, and fifteen days), but there may be exceptions to the time limit; for example, in the case of fraud or a clerical error.

It is important to review your earnings record at least every three years. Social Security has just made this a lot easier by mailing every worker over 25 a statement of their earning once a year. This program just began, but you should get the statement about three months before your birthday. You may also request that it be sent to you.

Q I am an 18-year-old college student, and I have lost my Social Security card. I was wondering if you could give me some information such as a telephone number that I could call to get a new one. I am sorry for the simplicity of my question, but any help you could offer would be much appreciated. Thank you very much for your time.

A Don't apologize for simple questions; usually the smartest people ask them. You may call Social Security at 800-772-1213 nationwide, toll free. But leave yourself a good chunk of time to get through. You may also visit your local Social Security office, but make sure you take an ID with you.

Q People are asking for your Social Security number for everything now. I was even asked for it to rent a movie, but refused to give it to them. Please tell me who has the right to request the number. For those who do not have the right to request it, do they have the right to refuse me service, credit, etc., if I don't give it to them?

A Social Security numbers may be used by anyone for lawful purposes. Some non-Social Security organizations are authorized specifically to use Social Security numbers, such as banks, state government agencies, parent locator services, other federal agencies, etc. Other users, such as the video store, may request your number for a lawful purpose, such as identifying customers and keeping records, but you may refuse to give it. However, the store can refuse to do business with you.

The Social Security number has become a sort of national registration number, and there's really nothing we can do about it. But I'm sure you know that you should be careful who you give the number to, because it can be misused in many ways, including *identity theft*, which is when a criminal sets up accounts in your name and the next thing you know, you're listed as a deadbeat or worse.

Q Hello. Could you please advise me how to get an estimate on how much I have paid into my Social Security? What website do you recommend?

A Yes. You can request a Social Security Statement online through the Social Security website at **www.ssa.gov**. Look for the "Online Services" section and click on the SS Statement request.

Q My problem is I have been looking for my daughter who is away at a college somewhere in the United States. She has neither contacted us for any type of financial assistance nor has she had any contact with her family. We are very concerned as to her whereabouts. All we have as far as ID is her Social Security number and name. If there is a way of locating her with this information, please let me know.

A Social Security will not disclose the whereabouts of someone, but will forward a letter from you if there are special circumstances, such as humanitarian or financial reasons. Where a parent seeks to contact a child, it is considered to be for a humanitarian purpose. Additionally, Social Security must be satisfied that the missing person would want to know about the contents of the letter.

The disappearance was far enough in the past (several months at least) to expect that Social Security would have a mailing address; and all other possibilities for contacting the missing person have been exhausted. If a child seeks a parent, they will inform the parent that the child is seeking the contact. You should go to your local Social Security office and ask about this. If the interviewer does not know about this policy, ask to speak to a supervisor.

Glossary

B

benefit estimates. The Social Security Administration will provide an estimate of the amount of benefits payable to any person who requests it. Benefit estimates are given based on the amount of earnings actually shown on the record of earnings and are not be based on any proposed future earnings.

black lung benefits. The federal Coal Mine Health and Safety Act of 1969 established payments to coal miners who suffer from pneumoconiosis, as long as the claim was filed prior to July 1, 1973. Claims made after July 1, 1973, are under the jurisdiction of the Department of Labor.

blindness, statutory. A disability that requires a central vision acuity of 20/200 or less in the better eye with the use of glasses or the field of vision limited so that the widest diameter subtends an angle no greater than twenty degrees.

C

central office (CO). Main office of the Social Security Administration. It is located in Baltimore, Maryland, and it issues all regulations and instructions to the district offices. It also interprets the law and issues policy statements.

claims representative. The person who is responsible for knowing about all aspects of the Social Security regulations. This person both represents the Social Security Administration and assists claimants who are making claims under the Social Security program.

combined checks. If two or more people who live in the same household receive benefits on the same account, the Social Security Administration will usually combine payments for each beneficiary into one monthly check.

compromise settlements. If the Social Security Administration overpays a beneficiary by less than $20,000, it may accept less than the total overpayment in full settlement. If this is the case, then there will be no further recovery of the balance.

contributions. Payroll taxes that are taken out of one's paycheck for Social Security.

D

date of entitlement. The date when a person becomes eligible for the payment of the monthly disability benefits.

date of onset. The date when a disability begins.

disability, cessation of. Occurs when the Social Security Administration determines that a person is no longer totally disabled within the definition of disability for Social Security purposes.

disability, permanent. A disability that is expected to last for at least twelve (12) months or result in death.

disability, termination. Occurs two months after cessation of disability.

disability, total. A disability that renders a person unable to perform *any* kind of work activity, considering one's age, education, and work experience.

district manager. Highest authority in each district office. The manager's duties are generally administrative, including maintaining personnel records and making sure that the office work is done.

Division of International Operations (DIO). The office that handles cases where the beneficiaries reside outside of the United States.

E

early retirement. A person can begin receiving his or her Social Security retirement benefits before full retirement age—62 being the earliest—but his or her benefit amount will be permanently reduced.

earnings test. The way one's earning affects Social Security retirement benefits. All beneficiaries, except those whose benefits are based on disability or are over full retirement age, are subject to a loss of benefits if their earnings exceed certain limits.

F

field offices. Collective title for over 1,300 district and branch offices of the Social Security Administration located throughout the United States.

full retirement age. The age at which a person can retire and collect full retirement benefits through Social Security. The exact age depends on the year of a person's birth.

H

health insurance. Federal health insurance program for certain eligible groups of people, including people 65 years of age and older and certain people below this age with a disability.

hospital insurance. Primarily pays for eligible in-patient care under Medicare.

I

initial determination. A formal decision affecting benefits, a period of disability, a person's earnings record, or one's entitlement to Medicare. Can be appealed.

insured status. Workers must have enough work credits in order to receive a benefit.

L

lump sum death payment. An amount of money payable to certain survivors of a worker who died fully or currently insured. It is only paid to one person.

M

medical insurance. Primarily pays for eligible doctors' bills under Medicare.

Medicare. *See health insurance.*

monthly earnings test. If a person is an employee of a company, there will be a nonservice month for any month after entitlement in which that person earns under a certain amount. Benefits are not withheld from a nonservice month.

O

Office of Central Records Operations (OCRO). The office that handles the information necessary to perform the duties of the Social Security Administration. Its duties include the assigning of Social Security numbers to workers, keeping track of changes of names on Social Security records, and maintaining the records of earning reported by employers for each individual Social Security number.

Office of Disability Operations (ODO). The office that handles cases of disability benefits.

overpayment, deduction. This occurs when the beneficiary is legally entitled to benefits, but for some reason, some or all of the benefits should not have been paid.

overpayment, entitlement. This occurs when a person files for benefits and the Social Security Administration pays the benefits, but later discovers that the person was never actually eligible for them in the first place.

P

Programs Operations Manual System (POMS). The rulebook used by all Social Security Administration district office personnel. It provides the working rules and interpretations of the laws and regulations.

R

regional offices. Social Security Administration offices in each of the ten regions of the United States.

S

Social Security Act. Federal legislation that provides for the payment of monthly benefits to retired and disabled workers and their dependents, and to certain survivors of covered workers who are deceased.

Social Security Administration (SSA). One of the largest government agencies in the country. It has the duty of administering several provisions of the Social Security Act.

Social Security benefits. Monthly payments for retired workers, disabled workers, and the survivors of covered workers.

statement of earnings. Statement that shows the annual earnings credited to a person's record.

Supplemental Security Income (SSI). A federal welfare program that was designed to provide a minimum amount of income to individuals regardless of their work and earnings under Social Security. Payable to the aged, blind, and disabled who are in financial need.

survivor benefits. Benefits payable to survivors of deceased workers. They are awarded to the aged widows, disabled widows, young mothers, surviving divorced wives, and children of deceased workers. An outdated but unchanged law that applies to female and underage survivors only.

T

teleservice centers (TSCs). Centers set up by the Social Security Administration designed to handle telephone inquiries from members of the public.

trial work period. When a disability beneficiary attempts to return to work, this is the time when his or her earnings will not be used to terminate his or her entitlement to disability benefits. Typically, a person can work for nine (9) months before Social Security will consider terminating his or her benefits.

U

unsuccessful work attempt. If a person is disabled and returns to work, but then stops again because of the disability, if that period of time was less than three months, then it is considered an unsuccessful work attempt.

W

waiting period. The first five full months of disability, when no benefits are available.

Appendix A:
List of FICA Yearly Maximums

FICA Yearly Maximums
(Maximum Earnings Subject to Social Security Tax)

Year	Earnings
1937 through 1950	$ 3,000
1951 through 1954	3,600
1955 through 1958	4,200
1959 through 1965	4,800
1966 through 1967	6,600
1968 through 1971	7,800
1972	9,000
1973	10,800
1974	13,200
1975	14,100
1976	15,300
1977	16,500
1978	17,700
1979	22,900
1980	25,900
1981	29,700
1982	32,400
1983	35,700

Year	Earnings
1984	37,800
1985	39,600
1986	42,000
1987	43,800
1988	45,000
1989	48,000
1990	51,300
1991	53,400
1992	55,500
1993	57,600
1994	60,600
1995	61,200
1996	62,700
1997	65,400
1998	68,400
1999	72,600
2000	76,200
2001	80,400
2002	84,900
2003	87,000
2004	87,900
2005	90,000
2006	94,200
2007	97,500

Future maximums will be increased based on the rate of inflation and announced by the Social Security Administration in the fall of the preceding year.

> ➤**NOTE:** The total FICA tax is 15.3% (half paid by the employer and half paid by the employee), of which 12.4% is for Old Age, Survivor, and Disability Insurance. It is only this portion of the tax that is subject to the limits stated in this appendix. There is no maximum for earnings subject to the hospital insurance (Medicare) portion of the FICA tax, which is 2.9%, payable one-half by the employer and half by the employee.

Appendix B:
Earnings Limits by Year

Year	Age	Monthly	Yearly
1992	Under 65	$620	$ 7,440
	65 and Older	850	10,200
1993	Under 65	640	7,680
	65 and Older	880	10,560
1994	Under 65	670	8,040
	65 and Older	930	11,160
1995	Under 65	680	8,160
	65 and Older	940	11,280
1996	Under 65	690	8,280
	65 and Older	1041	12,500
1997	Under 65	720	8640
	65 and Older	1125	13,500
1998	Under 65	760	9,120
	65 and Older	1208	14,500
1999	Under 65	800	9,600
	65 and Older	1291	15,500
2000	Under 65	840	10,080
	65 and Older	1416	17,000

Year	Age	Monthly	Yearly
2001	Under 65	890	10,680
	65 and Older	2083	25,000
2002	Under 65	940	11,280
	65 and Older	2500	30,000
2003	Under FRA	960	11,520
	FRA	2,560	30,720
2004	Under FRA	970	11,640
	FRA	2,590	31,080
2005	Under FRA	1,000	12,000
	FRA	2,650	31,800
2006	Under FRA	1,040	12,480
	FRA	2,770	33,240
2007	Under FRA	1,080	12,960
	FRA	2,870	34,440

*FRA=Full Retirement Age

Appendix C: Social Security Administration Resources

Social Security Administration's main website:
www.ssa.gov

To find the nearest Social Security Administration office:
800-772-1213
http://www.ssa.gov/locator/

To obtain an SS-5 form:
www.ssa.gov/online/ss-5.html

To request a statement:
www.ssa.gov/mystatement

To download the direct deposit form:
www.ssa.gov/deposit/

To report fraud:
800-269-0271

To estimate Social Security:
http://www.ssa.gov/planners/calculators.htm

Medicare Information
www.medicare.gov

National Organization of
   Social Security Claimant's Representatives
      800-431-2804
      www.nosscr.org

Federal Trade Commission ID Theft Hotline
      877-438-4338

Social Security Benefits Handbook
      by Stanley A. Tomkiel, III, Esq.
      www.socialsecuritybenefitshandbook.com

Appendix D:
Quarters of Coverage Required for Insured Status

Following is a chart showing the earnings required for a quarter of coverage and four charts that show the minimum number of *quarters of coverage* needed for Insured Status, according to the type of benefit.

Chart 1: Earnings Required for a Quarter of Coverage

Year	Amount
Pre-1978	$ 50
1978	250
1979	260
1980	290
1981	310
1982	340
1983	370
1984	390
1985	410
1986	440
1987	460
1988	470
1989	500
1990	520
1991	540
1992	570
1993	590
1994	620
1995	630

Year	Amount
1996	640
1997	670
1998	700
1999	740
2000	780
2001	830
2002	970
2003	890
2004	900
2005	920
2006	970
2007	1,000

(If you have access to the Internet, you may check online at **www.socialsecuritybenefitshandbook.com** for later years.)

Chart 2: Number of Quarters Required for Insured Status for Disability or Survivor Benefits

(For People Born in 1930 or Later)

Age of Onset of Disability or Death Required	Minimum Number of Quarters of Coverage
28 and younger	6
29	7
30	8
31	9
32	10
33	11
34	12
35	13
36	14
37	15
38	16
39	17
40	18
41	19
42	20
43	21
44	22
45	23
46	24
47	25
48	26
49	27
50	28
51	29

52	30
53	31
54	32
55	33
56	34
57	35
58	36
59	37
60	38
61	39
62 and older	40

Chart 3: Disability Insured Status

(see Sec. 604)

NOTE: *This chart shows the minimum number of quarters of coverage required in the calendar quarters immediately preceding onset of disability. For example, 15/30 means that 15 quarters of coverage are needed in the 30 calendar quarters (7 1/2 years) before onset of disability; 20/40 means that 20 quarters of coverage are needed in the 40 calendar quarters before onset of disability (10 years).*

Age at Onset of Disability	Minimum Number of Quarters of Coverage Required/Calendar Quarters Before Disability
24 and younger	6/12
24 1/2	7/14
25	8/16
25 1/2	9/18
26	10/20
26 1/2	11/22
27	12/24
27 1/2	13/26
28	14/28
28 1/2	15/30
29	16/32
29 1/2	17/34
30	18/36
30 1/2	19/38
31	20/40

Appendix E: Sample Benefit Amounts

*Worker with steady earnings at the **maximum** level since age 22*

Retirement at Beginning of Year	Retirement at Age 62	Retirement at Full Retirement Age	Retirement at Age 70
	Monthly Benefit	Monthly Benefit	Monthly Benefit
2000	$1,248	$1,433	$1,751
2001	$1,314	$1,536	$1,877
2002	$1,382	$1,660	$1,988
2003	$1,412	$1,721	$2,045
2004	$1,422	$1,784	$2,111
2005	$1,452	$1,874	$2,252
2006	$1,530	$1,961	$2,420
2007	$1,598	$1,998	$2,672

(Check online at **www.socialsecuritybenefitshandbook.com** for later years.)

*Worker with steady earnings at the **high** level since age 22*

Retirement at Beginning of Year	Retirement at Age 62	Retirement at Full Retirement Age	Retirement at Age 70
	Monthly Benefit	Monthly Benefit	Monthly Benefit
2000	$1,115	$1,279	$1,553
2001	$1,169	$1,364	$1,658
2002	$1,224	$1,467	$1,747
2003	$1,242	$1,512	$1,785
2004	$1,245	$1,559	$1,831

(Check online at **www.socialsecuritybenefitshandbook.com** for later years.)

*Worker with steady earnings at the **average** level since age 22*

Retirement at Beginning of Year	Retirement at Age 62	Retirement at Full Retirement Age	Retirement at Age 70
	Monthly Benefit	Monthly Benefit	Monthly Benefit
2000	$858	$987	$1,212
2001	$897	$1,051	$1,291
2002	$935	$1,126	$1,357
2003	$947	$1,157	$1,386
2004	$947	$1,190	$1,420

(Check online at **www.socialsecuritybenefitshandbook.com** for later years.)

*Worker with steady earnings at the **low** level since age 22*

Retirement at Beginning of Year	Retirement at Age 62	Retirement at Full Retirement Age	Retirement at Age 70
	Monthly Benefit	Monthly Benefit	Monthly Benefit
2000	$521	$598	$729
2001	$544	$636	$776
2002	$568	$682	$815
2003	$575	$701	$922
2004	$575	$721	$852

(Check online at **www.socialsecuritybenefitshandbook.com** for later years.)

Appendix F: Reduction Factors
(see Sec. 703)

The full retirement age (i.e., the age at which one may receive an unreduced retirement, spouse's, or widow's benefit) has been increased effective with those born in 1938 and later (1940 for widows) on a gradually increasing basis. (See Sec. 703 *Reductions* for a full discussion.) Therefore, additional reduction months are applied to those turning 62 (60 for widows) in 2000. For retirement and spouse's benefits, the reduction factor for reduction months in excess of 36 is 5/12 of 1 percent for each extra month.

Chart 1: Retirement Benefits

Reduction Months	Reduction Factor	Reduction Months	Reduction Factor	Reduction Months	Reduction Factor
1	.994	13	.927	25	.861
2	.988	14	.922	26	.855
3	.983	15	.916	27	.850
4	.977	16	.911	28	.844
5	.972	17	.905	29	.838
6	.966	18	.900	30	.833
7	.961	19	.894	31	.827
8	.955	20	.888	32	.822
9	.950	21	.883	33	.816
10	.944	22	.877	34	.811
11	.938	23	.872	35	.805
12	.933	24	.866	36	.800

Chart 2: Spouse's Benefits

Reduction Months	Reduction Factor	Reduction Months	Reduction Factor	Reduction Months	Reduction Factor
1	.993	13	.909	25	.826
2	.986	14	.902	26	.819
3	.979	15	.895	27	.812
4	.972	16	.888	28	.805
5	.965	17	.881	29	.798
6	.958	18	.875	30	.791
7	.951	19	.868	31	.784
8	.944	20	.861	32	.777
9	.937	21	.854	33	.770
10	.930	22	.847	34	.763
11	.923	23	.840	35	.756
12	.916	24	.833	36	.750

Chart 3: Widow(er)'s Benefits

Unlike retirement and spouse's benefits, the widow(er)'s reduction is limited to 28.5%. This requires a different fraction depending on the year of attainment of full retirement age (FRA). For widow(er)s, the primary insurance benefit is reduced by a fraction of the PIA for each reduction month according to the following chart.

Date of Birth	FRA	FRACTION
Through 1/1/40	65	$\frac{19}{40}$
1/2/40 – 1/1/41	65 + 2	$\frac{57}{124}$
1/2/41 – 1/1/42	65 + 4	$\frac{57}{128}$
1/2/42 – 1/1/43	65 + 6	$\frac{19}{44}$
1/2/43 – 1/1/44	65 + 8	$\frac{57}{136}$
1/2/44 – 1/1/45	65 + 10	$\frac{57}{140}$
1/2/45 – 1/1/57	66	$\frac{19}{48}$
1/2/57 – 1/1/58	66 + 2	$\frac{57}{148}$
1/2/58 – 1/1/59	66 + 4	$\frac{57}{152}$
1/2/59 – 1/1/60	66 + 6	$\frac{19}{52}$
1/2/60 – 1/1/61	66 + 8	$\frac{57}{160}$
1/2/61 – 1/1/62	66 + 10	$\frac{57}{164}$
1/2/62 or later	67	$\frac{19}{56}$

Appendix G:
Cost of Living Increases

Cost-of-Living Allowance (COLA) increases are applicable for benefits paid in the year indicated in the chart. The effective month of COLA increases is December of the year preceding, and the increase affects benefits payable beginning January of the indicated year.

Year	Percentage
1992	3.7%
1993	3.0%
1994	2.6%
1995	2.8%
1996	2.6%
1997	2.9%
1998	2.1%
1999	1.31%
2000	2.4%
2001	2.6%
2002	1.4%
2003	2.1%
2005	2.7%
2006	4.1%
2007	3.3%

(If you have access to the Internet, you may check online at **www.socialsecuritybenefitshandbook.com** for later years.)

Appendix H: Most Common Beneficiary Identification Codes

A:	Retirement on Own Work Record
B:	Aged Wife
B1:	Aged Husband
B2:	Young Wife (with Child in Care)
B6:	Divorced Wife
C:	Child
D:	Aged Widow
D1:	Aged Widower
D6:	Surviving Divorced Wife
E:	Young Widow (mother)
E1:	Surviving Divorced Mother
E4:	Young Widower (father)
F:	Parent
G:	Lump Sum Claimant
HA:	Disabled Worker
HB:	Aged Wife of Disabled Worker
HB2:	Young Wife of Disabled Worker
HC:	Child of Disabled Worker
J:	Prouty (special age 72 benefits)
K:	Prouty (wife)
M:	Medicare—Medical Insurance Only
T:	Medicare Only—Both Parts
W:	Disabled Widow
W1:	Disabled Widower
W6:	Surviving Disabled Divorced Wife

Appendix I:
Chart Summarizing the Effect
Between Beneficiaries
(see Sec. 904)

Type of Beneficiary	Effect of Marriage to Another Beneficiary
Type I	

Retired Worker (see Sec. 202)
Disabled Worker (see Sec. 203)
Widow(er) (see Sec. 204.4)
Disabled Widow(er) (see Sec. 204.6)
Surviving Divorced Spouse
  (divorced widow(er))
  (see Sec. 204.7)
Disabled Surviving Divorced
  Spouse (divorced widow(er))
  (see Sec. 204.7)
	No effect, benefits continue.

Type II	
Divorced Spouse (see Sec. 204.3) Parent (see Sec. 206)	Benefits terminate if marriage is to a retired or disabled worker, or a child under 18 or in school; if marriage is to any other beneficiary, benefits continue.

Type III

Mother/Father (young widow(er)) (see Sec. 204.5) Divorced Mother/Father (see Sec. 204.7) Disabled Adult Child (see Sec. 213)	Benefits terminate if marriage to a child under 18 or in school (child's benefits also terminate); if marriage is to any other beneficiary, benefits continue.

Type IV

Child under 18 or in School (see Secs. 205.1–205.2)	Benefits terminate upon remarriage to anyone.

Appendix J: Delayed Retirement Credits

The amount of a *delayed retirement credit* is calculated as a percentage of the primary insurance amount, based on the number of months no benefit is received after full retirement age. The percentages listed are annual. The credit for each month is $\frac{1}{12}$ of the annual figure. The amount of the credit is based on year of birth.

Year of Birth	Annual Credit
1917–24	3%
1925–26	3.5%
1927–28	4.0%
1929–30	4.5%
1931–32	5%
1933–34	5.5%
1935–36	6%
1937–38	6.5%
1939–40	7.0%
1941–42	7.5%
1943 and later	8.0%

Appendix K:
Medicare Premiums and
Deductibles for 2007

Hospital Insurance
  Premium—Part A

Free if you have 40 quarters of coverage.
$226/mo if you have 30-39 quarters.
$410/mo if you have less than 30 quarters.

Hospital Insurance—Part A

Co-Payments
  First 60 Days (Total) $992
  61st-90th Day (per day) $248
  Lifetime Reserve (per day) $496

Skilled Nursing Care
  20-100th day (per day) $124

Medical Insurance
  Premium—Part B

Beginning in 2007, this premium is based on income according to the chart on page 208.

You Pay	If Your Yearly Income Is	
	Single	*Married Couple*
$93.50	$80,000 or less	$160,000 or less
$105.80	$80,001-$100,000	$160,001-$200,000
$124.40	$100,001-$150,000	$200,001-$300,000
$142.90	$150,001-$200,000	$300,001-$400,000
$161.40	Above $200,000	Above $400,000

You Pay	If You Are Married but You File a Separate Tax Return From Your Spouse and Your Yearly Income Is
$93.50	Under $80,000 or less
$142.90	$80,001-$120,000
$161.40	Above $120,000

Medical Insurance—Part B
  Yearly Deductible $131

(Check online at **www.socialsecuritybenefitshandbook.com** for later years.)

Index

About the Author

Stanley A. Tomkiel III received his B.A. from Manhattan College in New York City and his J.D. from Western New England College School of Law in Springfield, Massachusetts. He is admitted to practice in both New York and Florida. Mr. Tomkiel was formerly employed by the Social Security Administration as a claims representative in various district offices in the Northeast.